TROUT

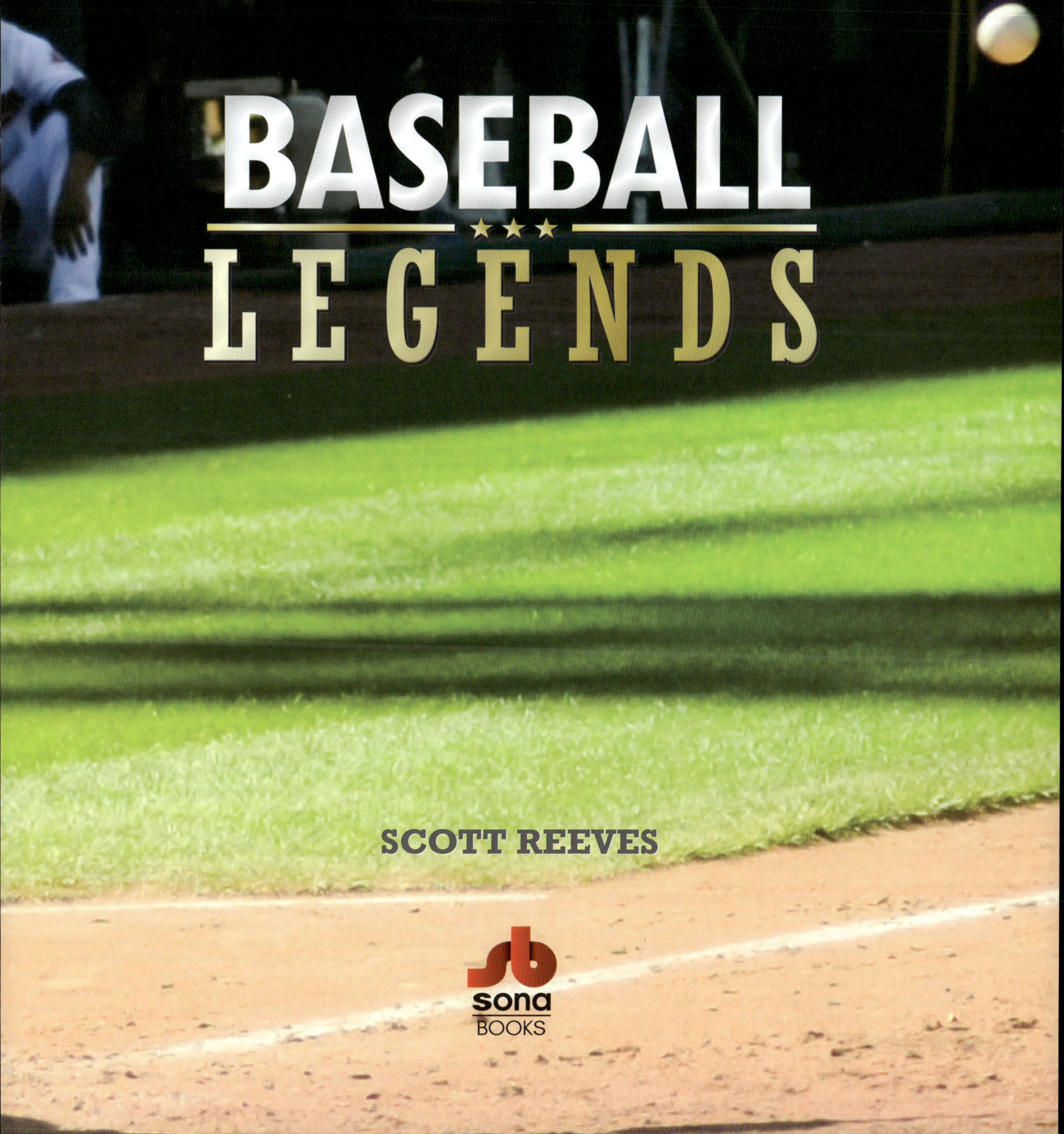

BASEBALL LEGENDS

SCOTT REEVES

sona BOOKS

First published in the UK by Sona Books, an imprint of Danann Media Publishing Limited

CAT NO. SON0617

Photography courtesy of
Getty images, Alamy and Wiki Commons

Dedicated to the memory of Michael and Thomas Tarmey

Project editor: Martin Corteel
Book design: Kevin Gardner
Proof reader: Cameron Thurlow
Cover design: Darren Grice

Printed in E.U.

ISBN: 978-1-915343-89-5

CONTENTS

INTRODUCTION 8

LEGENDS OF BASEBALL 10

ALBERT PUJOLS 12
JOE JACKSON 14
PEDRO MARTÍNEZ 18
BABE RUTH 20
KEN GRIFFEY JR 26
TY COBB 28
GREG MADDUX 32
JOE DIMAGGIO 34
ROGER CLEMENS 40
TED WILLIAMS 42
MICKEY MANTLE 46
JACKIE ROBINSON 48
RICKEY HENDERSON 54
WILLIE MAYS 56
SATCHEL PAIGE 60
ROBERTO CLEMENTE 62
STAN MUSIAL 68
HANK AARON 70
LOU GEHRIG 74
BARRY BONDS 76
WALTER JOHNSON 82
MIKE TROUT 84
CY YOUNG 88

50 GREATEST MLB PLAYERS 90

10 GREATEST TEAMS OF ALL TIME 108

10 GREATEST MANAGERS OF ALL TIME 120

10 GREATEST SERIES OF ALL TIME 130

INTRODUCTION

The New York Yankees have the most World Series titles in baseball

Professional baseball began in 1869 with the founding of the first pro team, the Cincinnati Red Stockings. Seven years later, several baseball teams came together to form the National League, and its first fixture – Boston at the Philadelphia Athletics – has been retroactively pegged as the first game in Major League Baseball, or MLB. Since then, tens of thousands of baseball players have competed in the quest to be named the country's best. For the first few decades of the National League, the team that topped the standings was considered the national champion. In 1903, the National League merged with the upstart American League. From then on, each league's champion faced off in a postseason series, giving birth to the World Series.

Baseball quickly proved popular. Americans flocked to support their local teams and baseball was designated as America's national pastime. Baseball players became celebrities. Newspapers sent reporters to follow the teams across the country. Play-by-play radio broadcasts helped fans feel part of the action. Everybody knew the biggest stars of their day. Some have since fallen into obscurity, remembered only by baseball historians and stats geeks. Others have shifted beyond the ballpark to become well-known sports stars around the world.

In this book, we'll celebrate legendary players in baseball's long history. We'll discover what made Willie Mays and Babe Ruth the greatest of all time, but we'll also explore the enduring legacies left behind by players like Roberto Clemente and Jackie Robinson. After that, we'll relive the best series, the sport's eminent managers and its most talented teams. Pick up a bat and get let's swinging!

Americans flocked to support their local teams and baseball was designated as America's national pastime.

LEGENDS OF BASEBALL

America's ballparks have played host to many big hitters and flame-throwing pitchers over 150 years of the major leagues. Some were pioneers of the game, others encapsulated a particular era. Some carried their teams to championships, others never earned a World Series ring. Many were simply the best at their specialism in the sport. With that in mind, it's time to discover what makes an otherwise great player into a baseball legend. Do suspicions of performance-enhancing drugs disqualify an outstanding player? How far was Babe Ruth's career derailed by alcohol? And can a player's cultural influence away from the ballpark contribute to their legendary status?

Some were pioneers of the game, others encapsulated a particular era.

Willie Mays was a perennial MVP contender who's remembered as baseball's greatest all-rounder

ALBERT PUJOLS

The Machine

Pujols rose high from tough beginnings. Born in the Dominican Republic, he was blooded in the game thanks to his softball pitcher father – but Pujols also had to help his dad home when he drank too much after games, and often had to practise using limes as balls and a milk carton glove. After moving to the United States, Pujols witnessed a shooting in Washington Heights, New York which led to his family relocating to Missouri. When he became old enough to interest MLB scouts, they had doubts due to his age and stature – though Tampa Bay scout Fernando Arango was so convinced in Pujols' ability that he quit after the Devil Rays passed on him. Pujols eventually slipped to the 402nd pick of the 1999 MLB draft.

Only when he made his MLB debut in 2001 did Pujols finally turn things around. First baseman Mark McGwire was one of the first to spot Pujols' talent – he told manager Tony La Russa that he'd be making a huge mistake if he didn't promote the youngster to the roster. La Russa listened, and Pujols had one of the greatest

Over the subsequent 21 years, Pujols' consistent swing helped him and the Cardinals to win two World Series.

Only three players have hit more home runs than Pujols in MLB history

rookie seasons in MLB history. Playing either third base, right field, left field or first base, Pujols recorded a .329 batting average with 37 home runs and 112 total runs.

Over the subsequent 21 years, Pujols' consistent swing helped him and the Cardinals to win two World Series. He ended his time in the major leagues in 2022 with a .296 batting average, 3,384 hits (good enough for ninth in the all-time standings) and 703 home runs (fourth in the all-time standings). He was effective to the end, winning the Comeback Player of the Year award in his final season after returning to the Cardinals and slogging 24 home runs.

~ ALBERT PUJOLS ~

Teams: St Louis Cardinals (2001–11), Los Angeles Angels (2012–21), Los Angeles Dodgers (2021), St Louis Cardinals (2022)

Batting Average: .296

Hits: 3,384

Home Runs: 703

Runs Batted In: 2,218

World Series Wins: 2 (2006, 2011)

Pujols enjoyed one of the best debut seasons a rookie has ever played

JOE JACKSON

Shoeless Joe

~ JOE JACKSON ~

Teams: Philadelphia Athletics (1908-09), Cleveland Naps/ Indians (1910-15), Chicago White Sox (1915-20)

Batting Average: .356

Home Runs: 54

Runs Batted In: 792

World Series Wins: 1 (1917)

Jackson's lifetime batting average of .356 is the third highest in MLB history

On 1 October 1919, Joe Jackson took to Redland Field in Cincinnati for Game 1 of the World Series – and the Chicago White Sox star player seemed to relish the occasion. Over the next nine days, Jackson's White Sox took on the Cincinnati Reds in a series that seesawed between the two teams. Jackson made 12 base hits – a record that was not broken until 1964 – and led both teams with a .375 batting average. From his position in the outfield, he had no errors and threw out a runner at the plate. Nevertheless, Jackson's individual stats weren't enough to secure victory, and the Reds became MLB champions with a 5-3 series victory.

Part of the reason why the Reds won was that they hit three out of nine triples to Jackson's spot in left field – and that unusually high number would haunt him for the rest of his life. Jackson put the loss behind him and the White Sox got back to work in 1920, but Jackson's career soon came to a sudden halt amid accusations that he'd deliberately thrown the World Series.

Jackson's path to notoriety began in South Carolina. His family needed him to contribute to the coffers as soon as he was able. By the age of six, Jackson was working 12-hour shifts in the local textile mill, and a lack of formal schooling left him illiterate. In later years, Jackson tried to hide his lack of education. In restaurants, he'd pretend to read the menu and order what he heard his teammates ask for. When asked to sign memorabilia, he had his wife do it for him.

Jackson's natural athleticism caught the eye of his supervisors at the mill, and at the age of 13 he was asked to try out for the company baseball team. It was a great bonus for the family – not only was he was paid extra for representing the mill, but his brothers would shake down the crowd for tips when Jackson made a great play. To protect their young charge, the team manager used Jackson as a pitcher until one day when Jackson broke an opponent's arm with a fastball and nobody else wanted to bat against him. The manager agreed to pull Jackson from the mound and put him in the outfield. Jackson stayed there for the rest of his career. Now free to concentrate on batting, Jackson refined his technique

Jackson's path to notoriety began in South Carolina.

and proved to be even better at the plate than he was on the mound.

While Jackson played for the mill, a fan made a bat for Jackson using the tobacco-stained timber of a hickory tree. Jackson found the bat – which he named Black Betsy – was the perfect weight for him. Black Betsy followed Jackson for the rest of his career. So did a nickname that Jackson was given during a game when a new pair of boots troubled him. Jackson took off his footwear to bat and ran the bases in only his socks. 'Shoeless Joe' stuck with him for the rest of his life.

Jackson began to play semi-pro baseball in 1905 and was eventually scouted by the Philadelphia Athletics, but he didn't gel with manager Connie Mack. Jackson played only five games for the Athletics in both 1908 and 1909, and struggled to settle in the big city. Mack traded

Jackson's bat, Black Betsy, was sold for $577,610 on eBay in 2001

The New York Giants started left-handed pitchers in four of six games in the 1917 World Series in an attempt to neutralise Jackson

Jackson to the Cleveland Naps in 1910, and they put Jackson on the roster of the minor league New Orleans Pelicans. There, Jackson helped his team to the Southern Association pennant with a .387 batting average.

Jackson was ready for a proper run in the major leagues, and he was recalled by the Naps for the 1911 season. Still classed as a rookie since he'd only made 30 appearances across three prior MLB seasons, Jackson went on to set several rookie records over 147 games in 1911. His .408 batting average would have won the batting title almost any other year, but in 1911 Ty Cobb hit a staggering .419. Even so, Jackson had the best on-base percentage and finished fourth in the MVP voting. Thanks to Jackson's exploits, the Naps finished third in the American League, despite losing ace pitcher Addie Joss, who died of meningitis as the season began.

Jackson's rookie season batting average in 1911 was only beaten by Ty Cobb (left) and still stands as a franchise record

In 1912, Jackson batted .395 and led the American League in hits, triples and total bases. The following year, he led the league with 197 hits and smacked a ball out of New York's Polo Grounds. Jackson was recognised as a great batter, but his team didn't match his exploits. The Naps slumped to the bottom of the league in 1914, and being renamed the Cleveland Indians in 1915 didn't do much to help improve their form. Partway through 1915, when it was clear the Indians were far from competitive in the pennant race, new manager Lee Fohl decided to cash in his best chip. Jackson was traded to the Chicago White Sox for $31,500 and three players.

In Chicago, Jackson was part of a more competitive roster. He helped his new teammates to secure a third-place finish in 1915, then pushed them to second in 1916 with a team-best .341 batting average. In 1917, the White Sox went one better again. They dominated the American League with a 100-54 record (the highest win total in franchise history) and finished nine games in front of the Boston Red Sox. The White Sox completed their best-ever season with a 4-2 dismantling of a talented New York Giants side that made a crucial mistake in the field in Game 5 – Giants third baseman Heinie Zimmerman faced claims that he purposely allowed Eddie Collins to score the series-winning run. It wasn't the last time that rumours of fixing would tarnish the World Series.

The United States' entry into the First World War meant that baseball players were eligible for the draft. Jackson avoided overseas service by spending much of the 1918 season building battleships in a Delaware shipyard, but he was back in a baseball uniform in 1919 – and he was back at his best. His .351 batting average helped the White Sox rebound from an off year to finish top of the American League again. This time, their reward was a World Series against the Cincinnati Reds. But in the lead up to the postseason, several White Sox players were offered $5000 each to throw the World Series and allow the unfavoured Reds to win.

Babe Ruth said he modelled his swing on Jackson's, calling it the 'perfectest'

The level of Jackson's guilt and innocence in one of baseball's murkiest affairs is still contested today. Certainly, Jackson wasn't one of the ringleaders. Jackson reportedly turned down the deal – which would double his salary – on two occasions. The other seven players implicated in the scandal testified that Jackson wasn't present at their planning meetings. Jackson tried to arrange a meeting with White Sox owner Charles Comiskey to tell him about his concerns, but Comiskey refused to meet him.

Perhaps Jackson gave in when teammate Lefty Williams dropped a bag full of cash on Jackson's hotel room floor. During the eight games of the World Series, Jackson was the best batter – but there's some cause for suspicion. In the games that the White Sox played fair, Jackson had a .550 batting average. In the games the White Sox threw, his average dropped to .250. Was that a coincidence or evidence that Jackson didn't try as hard? There's also the unusually high number of triples hit to Jackson in the outfield. Did Jackson purposely drag his heels when fielding those balls?

In 1920, Jackson had one of his best seasons, batting .382.

In 1920, Jackson had one of his best seasons, batting .382 and setting his best marks for home runs and runs batted in. But it all came to an end in the final week of the season, when news leaked that a conspiracy to fix the 1919 World Series had been uncovered. Jackson was among eight White Sox players who were suspended pending an investigation. The illiterate Jackson was represented by the White Sox lawyer. It was a clear conflict of interest since the White Sox were keen to portray the fix as the action of a few bad eggs rather than evidence of a corrupt ball club. Nevertheless, a jury took just two hours to declare all eight players not guilty. That wasn't good enough for MLB Commissioner Kenesaw Mountain Landis, who was worried that the scandal could have a long-lasting detrimental effect on the sport. Despite the legal verdict, Landis slapped lifetime bans on all eight players. Jackson's MLB career was over.

Jackson tried to stay in the game. He played and managed a number of teams in Georgia and South Carolina, but always under assumed names. He later opened a liquor store. One day, legendary player Ty Cobb and a reporter decided to drop by. Jackson showed no sign of recognising the famous Cobb, until a disbelieving Cobb revealed his identity. 'Sure I know you, Ty,' Jackson replied. 'But I wasn't sure you wanted to know me. A lot of them don't.'

Jackson – like the other tainted players in what became known as the Black Sox Scandal – was exiled from the sport that he loved. But Jackson's reputation has been rehabilitated in recent years by fans and pundits who point out that his guilt is far from proven. Moves have been made to posthumously rescind Jackson's lifetime ban and make him eligible for the Hall of Fame. Whether or not Jackson gets a plaque at Cooperstown, it's clear that one of baseball's best early hitters left a positive mark on the game during the ten years before the 1919 World Series, and he should be remembered for more than just being the most famous member of the notorious Black Sox.

PEDRO MARTÍNEZ

The Pocket Rocket

Baseball statisticians rate Martínez as one of the greatest pitchers of all time

~ PEDRO MARTÍNEZ ~

Teams: Los Angeles Dodgers (1992–93), Montreal Expos (1994–97), Boston Red Sox (1998–2004), New York Mets (2005–08), Philadelphia Phillies (2009)

Win-Loss: 219–100

Earned Run Average: 2.93

Strikeouts: 3,154

World Series Wins: 1 (2004)

Small and skinny, Martínez had a path to the big leagues through his older brother. When Ramon Martínez signed with the Los Angeles Dodgers in 1984, his new club's scouts became aware that he had a talented little brother. Pedro signed for the Dodgers in 1988 and spent four years in the farm system while his coaches worked out whether the little guy had enough juice for the big leagues.

The Dodgers gave Martínez a chance near the end of 1992, asking him to play as a reliever from the bullpen, but the Dodgers traded Martínez away at the end of 1993 having decided he just wasn't big enough to be a dominant starter. The Expos had a different opinion. In Montreal, Martínez worked on his fastball and joined the starting rotation. He pitched nine perfect innings against the San Diego Padres in 1995 before allowing a hit in extra innings, was named to the All-Star Game in 1996, and went 17-8 with a National League-best 1.90 ERA in 1997. That gained Martínez his first Cy Young Award and his first major payday as he neared free agency.

It was the Boston Red Sox who waved their cheque book most. They traded for Martínez just seven days after he won the Cy Young Award and locked him up for the next seven seasons. Martínez ruled the roost at Fenway, despite it being one of the most hitter-friendly ballparks in the major leagues. He won the Cy Young Award again in 1999 and 2000, two seasons in which Martínez had a cumulative 41-10 record with 597 strikeouts and a 1.90 earned run average. In 2004, he helped the Red Sox win their first World Series in 86 years, pitching seven shutout innings in Game 3 in St Louis to give Boston a 3-0 lead in the World Series. Though his career fizzled out in New York and Philadelphia thanks to injury, Martínez still did enough to becoming the tenth pitcher to win 100 games in both leagues.

He won the Cy Young Award again in 1999 and 2000.

Martínez changed his fastball grip in Montreal and it instantly gave him more control

BABE RUTH

The Sultan of Swat

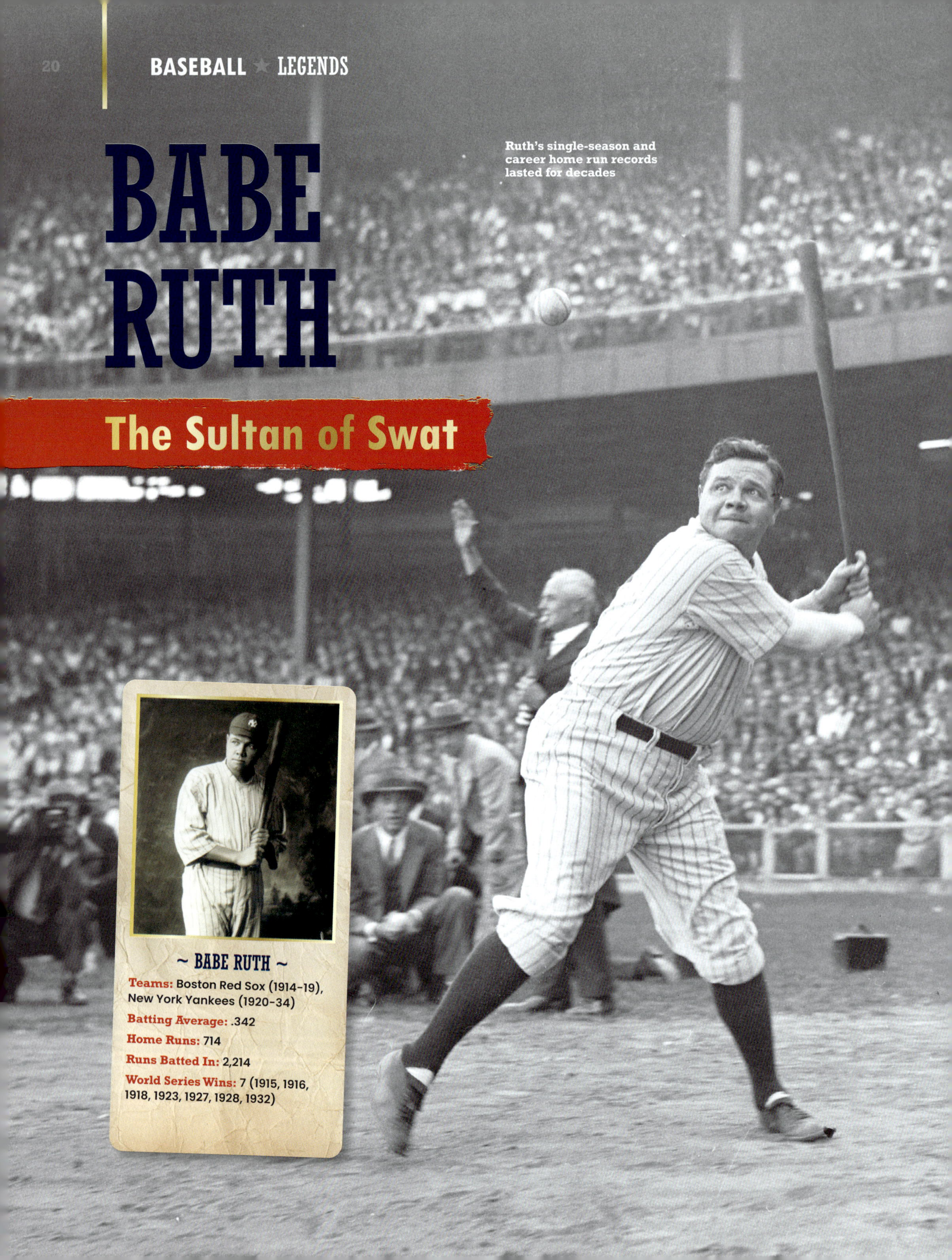

Ruth's single-season and career home run records lasted for decades

~ BABE RUTH ~

Teams: Boston Red Sox (1914-19), New York Yankees (1920-34)

Batting Average: .342

Home Runs: 714

Runs Batted In: 2,214

World Series Wins: 7 (1915, 1916, 1918, 1923, 1927, 1928, 1932)

The man who became known to the world as 'Babe' was born George Herman Ruth in Baltimore in 1895. He seems to have had a tough upbringing. Only one of Ruth's seven younger siblings survived infancy. Ruth was raised in a saloon with little parental discipline, skipped school, and often found himself in trouble with the law. By the age of seven, the authorities removed Ruth from his home and sent him to St Mary's Industrial School for Boys – a reformatory and orphanage for troubled kids.

Here, Ruth found the guidance he'd lacked so far. Brother Matthias, a Xaverian monk, encouraged Ruth to join the school's baseball practices. Brother Matthias was a stern teacher, but he was also strong and a good ballplayer – both traits that a young tearaway respected. Brother Matthias taught Ruth how to run the bases and hit a baseball, and Ruth would use the skills he learned from his unconventional first coach to fundamentally alter the sport.

In early 1914, St Mary's had a visitor: Jack Dunn, the owner and manager of the minor league Baltimore Orioles. He's heard about the talented youngsters in the reformatory and wondered whether any would do for his team. Dunn watched St Mary's take on another Xaverian school, Mount St Mary's College, and he was most impressed by the winning pitcher. That happened to be young George Ruth, who only started pitching because he found the tame efforts of his school friends to be so comical. Dunn signed 19-year-old Ruth to a contract with a $100 monthly wage and presented his new charge to the rest of the Orioles during spring training. They immediately christened their new teammate as Dunn's 'Babe'.

When the season started, Ruth proved himself to be a rare combination: a star pitcher and hard-hitting batter. He helped the Orioles to top the International League,

Ruth arrived in Boston on 11 July 1914. It was a successful first day.

Ruth may warrant a place in the Hall of Fame for his pitching talent alone

but they failed to pull in the crowds. Dunn was forced to sell his best players and touted Ruth across the leagues. The top bid for Ruth came from the Boston Red Sox, who took on Ruth's contract along with teammates Ernie Shore and Ben Egan.

Ruth arrived in Boston on 11 July 1914. It was a successful first day. In the morning, he met a waitress named Helen who'd go on to become his wife. In the afternoon, he pitched his first game at Fenway Park and beat the Cleveland Naps. After losing his second start, Ruth was rarely used for the rest of the season, making only five appearances. He didn't gel with his teammates either. They considered the newcomer to be cocky and brash. When Ruth declared he was a fine hitter who wanted to take batting practise, his teammates told the pitcher to stay in his lane. When the message didn't sink in and Ruth continued to bat in training, his teammates sawed his bats in half.

Ruth spent the bulk of 1914 helping a Red Sox farm team, the Providence Grays, win the International League pennant. He finally broke into the Red Sox starting rotation in 1915 and had an 18-8 regular season record, but he wasn't called to pitch in the 1915 World Series victory. In 1916, Ruth had a league-best 1.75 ERA and did pitch in the World Series – winning Game 2, a 14-inning marathon that remained the longest World Series game until 2005.

The United States' entry into the First World War had far-reaching ramifications – and among its lesser-known effects is how it transformed Babe Ruth's career. The Red Sox manager enlisted in the armed forces, and his replacement Ed Barrow had to plug several gaps on the roster at the start of the 1918 season. Recognising that Ruth was as talented with the bat as he was with the ball, Barrow decided to put Ruth into the outfield on days he wasn't pitching. Ruth quickly repaid his new manager's faith. He hit four home runs in consecutive games, including one off legendary pitcher Walter Johnson. By the end of the year, Ruth had a .300 batting average, 11 home runs (the joint highest total in the league) and a 13-7 pitching record with a 2.22 ERA. The Red Sox won a third World Series in four years, with Ruth pitching both Game 1 and Game 4.

Ruth was undoubtedly the best Red Sox player on both offense and defence, but Barrow found him increasingly difficult to control. Ruth almost lost Game 4 of the 1918 World Series due to poor pitching – the result of a play fight that damaged his throwing hand. He skipped 1919 spring training to hold out for an improved wage. He had a lackadaisical approach to timekeeping, often turning up late to training and breaking night-time curfews. He even fronted up to Barrow in the dressing room and challenged him to a fight.

At the end of a disappointing 1919, Red Sox owner Harry Frazee had endured Ruth's escapades for long enough. In need of cash to support his other business ventures, and sure that Ruth had a negative effect on clubhouse morale, Frazee agreed a $100,000 price for the troublesome pitcher-hitter with Jacob Ruppert, the owner of the New York Yankees.

Ruth's move to New York also saw him complete the move from pitcher to slugger

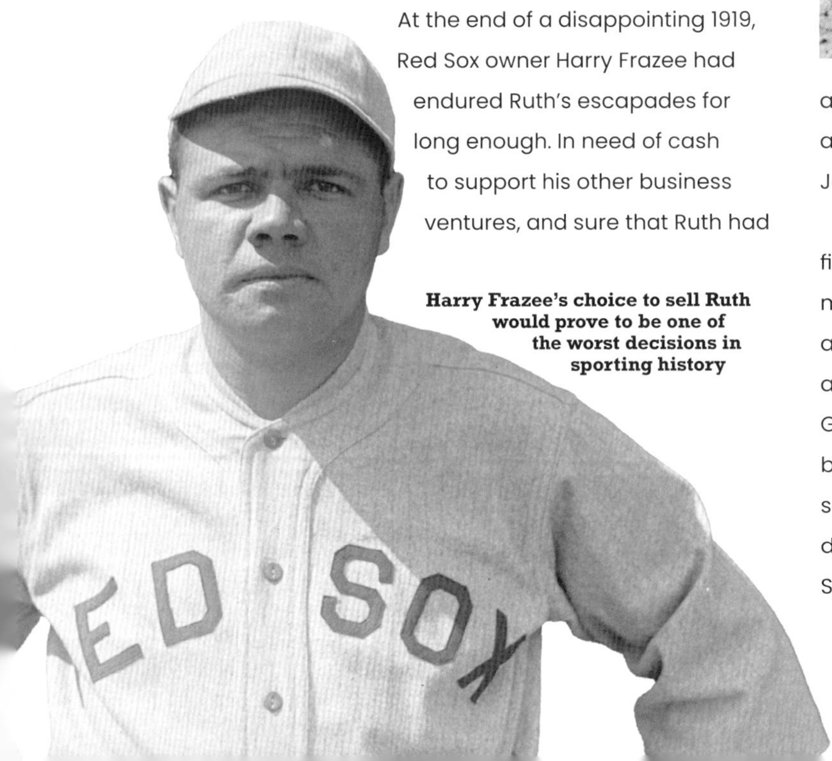

Harry Frazee's choice to sell Ruth would prove to be one of the worst decisions in sporting history

Ruppert pulled off the deal of the century, and Ruth's first year in New York was an eventful one. His new manager, Miller Huggins, told Ruth to ditch the pitching and concentrate purely on batting. Ruth responded with a huge slug on 1 May that sent the ball out of the Polo Grounds, a feat that had only been accomplished once before, by Shoeless Joe Jackson. Ruth hit 54 regular-season home runs, setting a new MLB record and almost doubling the total he set the previous year with the Red Sox. Ruth was helped by a new type of baseball that flew further and faster in the air. He also benefited when pitchers stopped throwing spitballs after Cleveland Indians shortstop Ray Chapman died following a hit to the head in August. No matter the cause, Ruth's unprecedented batting brought fans flocking to the ballpark. The Yankees became the first team to draw more than a million fans over the course of the season, and fans travelled hundreds of miles to see Ruth when the Yankees went on the road.

Ruth's explosive hitting shattered the dead-ball era and pioneered a new form of offensive hitting. Ruth broke his home run record again in 1921, hitting 59 homers with a joint career-best .378 batting average. That same season, he broke Roger Connor's record of 138 career home runs – and Ruth was just getting started. He hit another home run in the 1921 all-New York World Series – the Yankees' first postseason appearance – though they lost to the Giants. The same two clubs met in 1922 with the same result.

Ruth was still a handful in the clubhouse as well as on the diamond. He crashed his car in July 1920 with three teammates aboard, though didn't miss a game despite ending up upside down in a ditch. There's a chance that the accident was partly caused by alcohol since Ruth was known for drinking heavily after games. Ruth was also suspended for the start of the 1922 season after an unauthorised barnstorming trip after the 1921 World Series. Upon his return, he was ejected for throwing dust in an umpire's face and tried to climb into the stands to confront a heckler.

In 1923, the Yankees moved from the Polo Grounds to Yankee Stadium – and Ruth walloped a home run in the opening game. Yankee Stadium was designed with Ruth in mind, with a closer right fence that made it easier for left-handed batters to hit home runs, and it soon became dubbed 'the house that Ruth built'. Thanks to their new ground, the Yankees dominated the American League, winning the pennant by 17 games. Once again, the two New York teams faced off on the World Series. This time, Ruth left his mark on the postseason. He batted .368, walked eight times, scored eight runs and

Curse of the Bambino

When the Boston Red Sox sold Babe Ruth to the New York Yankees in 1919, they were the most successful major league franchise. The Red Sox won five of the first 15 World Series, including three with Ruth on the roster. After the departure of Ruth, the glory days suddenly came to an end. While the Yankees turned into the most dominant force in MLB, the Red Sox failed to top the American League until 1946.

They made four World Series appearances – 1946, 1967, 1975 and 1986 – but lost on each occasion. Bad luck plagued the team as fumbled plays, missed calls and other teams' results didn't go their way. It culminated in 1986, when the Red Sox had more than a 99 per cent chance of winning but still managed to pluck defeat from the jaws of victory. As the bad results piled on, fed-up Bostonians concluded their team suffered as a punishment for owner Harry Frazee choosing a quick payday over the best baseball player in history. Only in 2004 was the curse broken. Since then, the Red Sox have made up for lost time, winning the World Series again in 2007, 2013 and 2018.

The Curse of the Bambino lasted 86 years until the Red Sox defeated the St Louis Cardinals in 2004

The Called Shot

The Yankees and Chicago Cubs were tied 4-4 in Game 3 of the 1932 World Series when Ruth stepped to the plate in the fifth inning. The Chicago crowd had been on Ruth's back since the teams had warmed up, and their mood wasn't cheered when Ruth hit a three-run homer. Now, their hostility was turned up to max, and Ruth was fed up with the braying. With the pitch count at 2-2, Ruth pointed to the centre field bleachers. He may have been indicating to the Yankee dugout that he had one strike left.

He may have been heckling the Cubs bench. But the oft-repeated legend says that Ruth was pointing to where he was going to hit the next pitch. Charlie Root flung the ball, Ruth swung – and the ball flew to centre field, clearing the wall easily. It was one of the longest home runs ever hit at Wrigley Field, and Ruth chortled as he jogged around the bases, enjoying every second. The hit went down in baseball history as the 'called shot' – and Ruth was canny enough not to contradict the popular account.

The 1932 World Series wasn't a close affair – the Yankees swept the Cubs in four

hit three home runs to win his first World Series ring with the Yankees. There'd be more to come.

In 1924, the Yankees missed out on the World Series for the first time in four years – beaten to the pennant by the Senators. Ruth's 46 home runs were still the league's best, and he won his only batting title with a .378 batting average, matching his career-best mark from 1921. Ruth didn't lack effort in his attempt to knock the Senators from the top of the American League. He crashed into the outfield wall so hard during one game in Washington that he knocked himself out, and then refused to leave the game. The following year, Ruth also spent time as a hospital inpatient due to what sportswriters described as bellyache thanks to overconsumption of hot dogs and soda. More likely is that the Yankees insisted that Ruth seek treatment for alcohol dependency – or possibly a sexually transmitted infection resulting from dalliances on road trips. Whatever the diagnosis, Ruth played only 98 games and had his worst season as a Yankee, getting only 25 home runs with a .290 batting average.

In 1926, Ruth returned to his best, and Miller Huggins built a new, young Yankees line-up around his veteran star. The hard-hitting roster soon became known as Murderers' Row for the way they dominated opposing

Ruth hit an outfield fence so hard in Washington that he knocked himself out – but got up and completed the game

As Ruth's celebrity increased, he appeared in several movies – here with Gary Cooper

In early 1930, he signed a two-year contract worth $80,000 a year.

pitchers, and featured Lou Gehrig as the perfect follow-up man to Ruth in the batting line-up. Thanks to the fearsome duo, the Yankees returned to the World Series. Ruth hit three home runs in Game 4 – the first time it had been done in the World Series – but failed to steal base at a crucial moment in Game 7. The Yankees ultimately lost the World Series to the St Louis Cardinals but returned to the postseason and won rings in both 1927 and 1928. Those two championship teams are regularly named among the best teams of all time. Ruth broke his own single-season home run record in 1927 by smashing 60 home runs, pursued all the way by Gehrig. Ruth was on course to top it again in 1928 before he hit a rare batting slump.

Ruth was a fierce negotiator who was determined to get what he thought he was worth. In early 1930, he signed a two-year contract worth $80,000 a year – a salary more than twice as much as the next highest paid MLB player. He was probably worth it, though. Ruth bashed 49 home runs in 1930 and 46 in 1931 – the last time he'd lead the league in that category. In 1932, he earned his seventh and final World Series ring when the Yankees beat the Chicago Cubs, a series in which Ruth hit the 'called shot' – one of the most famous home runs in baseball history.

By 1935, Ruth was in the twilight of his career and his once-unmatchable numbers no longer led the league. Ruth expressed a desire to move into management, and although the Yankees had benefited from Ruth's play for more than a decade, they had no intention of letting a loose cannon like him take charge. Instead, Ruth was traded to the Boston Braves in 1935 on the understanding that he'd become player-manager – but the Braves soon regretted their decision, since Ruth was now a shadow of his former self. After an argument with the Braves owner, Ruth retired with immediate effect in June 1935.

Though his career ended with a fizzle rather than a bang, the Sultan of Swat left a profound legacy on baseball. When Ruth started playing, baseball was stuck in the dead-ball era. By the time Ruth left, batters aimed to blow the other team off the field with power hitting. Ruth almost single-handedly transformed baseball into America's game, and he became one of the few baseball players whose fame was blasted around the world at the speed of one of his legendary home runs.

Ruth's number three was retired by the Yankees in 1948, a few months before his death from cancer

KEN GRIFFEY JR

The Kid

To baseball fans who grew up in the 1990s, Ken Griffey Jr. is as much an icon as *Friends*, the Spice Girls and the Nintendo Game Boy. His first stint with the Mariners spanned the entire decade – Griffey was selected with the number-one pick of the 1987 draft and debuted on 3 April 1989, hitting a line-drive double in his first at-bat. A week later, in Griffey's first at-bat at his home stadium, he hit his first home run. So began Griffey's golden decade in Seattle. Between 1989 and 1999, he hit 398 home runs, batted in 1,152 runs, earned ten All-Star selections and ten Golden Gloves for his exceptional work in the field. He was a seven-time Silver Slugger and MVP in 1997, when he achieved career-best tallies in runs scored, home runs and runs batted in.

As baseball's biggest star in the 90s, Griffey was one of the first baseball players to take advantage of the commercialisation of sport. He signed lucrative endorsement deals with Nike and Nintendo, and his face looked out from the box of Wheaties breakfast cereal. Griffey was a natural choice for brands that wanted to reach the most people. He was young and cool. He debuted at 19, wore his cap backwards and was

Griffey's popularity helped baseball recover from the 1994 strike that dented the league's image

~ KEN GRIFFEY JR ~

Teams: Seattle Mariners (1989-99), Cincinnati Reds (2000-08), Chicago White Sox (2008), Seattle Mariners (2009-10)

Batting Average: .284

Hits: 2,781

Home Runs: 630

Runs Batted In: 1,836

World Series Wins: 0

So began Griffey's golden decade in Seattle.

phenomenally athletic. As if to emphasise his role as flag bearer for the next generation, Griffey even played two seasons with his father, Ken Senior, after the veteran followed his son to the Mariners in 1990.

After he left Seattle, Griffey's career began to be affected by injuries, but he still did enough to end his career with 630 home runs, the seventh-highest total of all time. Griffey was inducted into both the Mariners and Reds Halls of Fame, and in 2016, he was elected to the MLB Hall of Fame with a record 99.32% of the vote.

Griffey's speed and athleticism made him a perfect choice for centre field

TY COBB

The Georgia Peach

Tyrus 'Ty' Cobb made his MLB debut on 30 August 1905, hitting a double for the Detroit Tigers against the New York Highlanders in his first at-bat. Though Cobb seemed to be instantly at home at the plate, the debutant was actually an emotional wreck. Three weeks earlier, his mother had shot and killed his father at their Georgia home. Amanda Cobb was ultimately cleared of criminal charges after claiming she thought her husband was an intruder – but they'd been embroiled in marital strife, and Cobb must have been in turmoil as he wondered whether his mother was capable of murder.

To add to Cobb's difficulties, he was just 18 years old –

Cobb's style of hitting and running were perfect for the dead-ball era

~ TY COBB ~

Teams: Detroit Tigers (1905-27), Philadelphia Athletics (1927-28)

Batting Average: .366

Home Runs: 117

Runs Batted In: 1,944

World Series Wins: 0

To add to Cobb's difficulties, he was just 18 years old.

the youngest player in the major leagues by more than a year – and his veteran teammates took an instant dislike to the newcomer. They smashed Cobb's bats, hid his boots, soaked his clothes and tossed insults his way. Tigers manager Hughie Jennings allowed the hazing to continue, thinking it would toughen up Cobb. Although a cruel method of man-management, Jennings was satisfied with the result. Cobb developed a brutal and ruthless attitude that he carried throughout the rest of his career. In his own words, Cobb transformed into 'a snarling wildcat'.

Cobb became the first-choice Tigers centre fielder in his second season, batting .316 in 98 games. But Cobb was still just getting his eye in and adapting to the major leagues. In 1907, after shifting to right field, Cobb helped the Tigers to three consecutive American League pennants. Although they lost the World Series on each occasion (twice to the Chicago Cubs, once to the Pittsburgh Pirates), the Tigers were regularly pegged as the best team in the major leagues – and young Cobb was their best player.

During the Tigers' hat-trick of pennant-winning seasons, Cobb led the league in batting average, hits and runs batted in. Cobb had discovered the ingredients needed for success in the dead-ball era: hitting little and often, making good use of bunts, getting players on base and stealing base where possible. In 1907, Cobb managed to score a run by stealing second, third and home – he'd manage the unusual feat four times in his career, still an MLB record. Cobb's 1909 home run title illustrates the negligible impact home runs had in the dead-ball era. Cobb led the league with just nine home runs, and every single one was hit inside the park – making Cobb the only player in MLB history to win the home run title without clearing the fence.

Cobb's hard running often led to confrontations on the field, and he was never one to back down from a fight. In 1917 spring training, Cobb sparked a bench-clearing brawl after spiking Buck Herzog of the New York Giants. Cobb and Herzog continued the fight that evening in the hotel both teams were staying in. Cobb also got into an arranged fight with umpire Billy Evans under the stands after a game, with players from both teams forming a circle to watch. Perhaps the most notorious of all Cobb's fights came in 1912, when he assaulted a heckler in New York who'd been riding Cobb's back all game. Only when Cobb reached the fan in the stands did he realise that the man had lost a hand in a work accident – but so angry was Cobb that he still let the fan have it. The Tigers players protested the suspension that Cobb received for that incident and refused to play their next game. The subsequent 24-2 loss that the second-string Tigers suffered to the Philadelphia Athletics set a host of unwanted negative records, including hits allowed and runs allowed.

Cobb didn't just use his fists in the ballpark. In 1908, he received a suspended sentence for assaulting a labourer who complained when Cobb walked over his freshly laid asphalt. In 1909, he was arrested again for fighting with a hotel elevator operator and slashing the hotel watchman with a knife. Then, in 1912, Cobb suffered a minor stab wound during a fight with three intoxicated men who blocked his car in New York – though he was fit

Cobb's 98.2% on the 1936 Hall of Fame ballot was unsurpassed until 1992

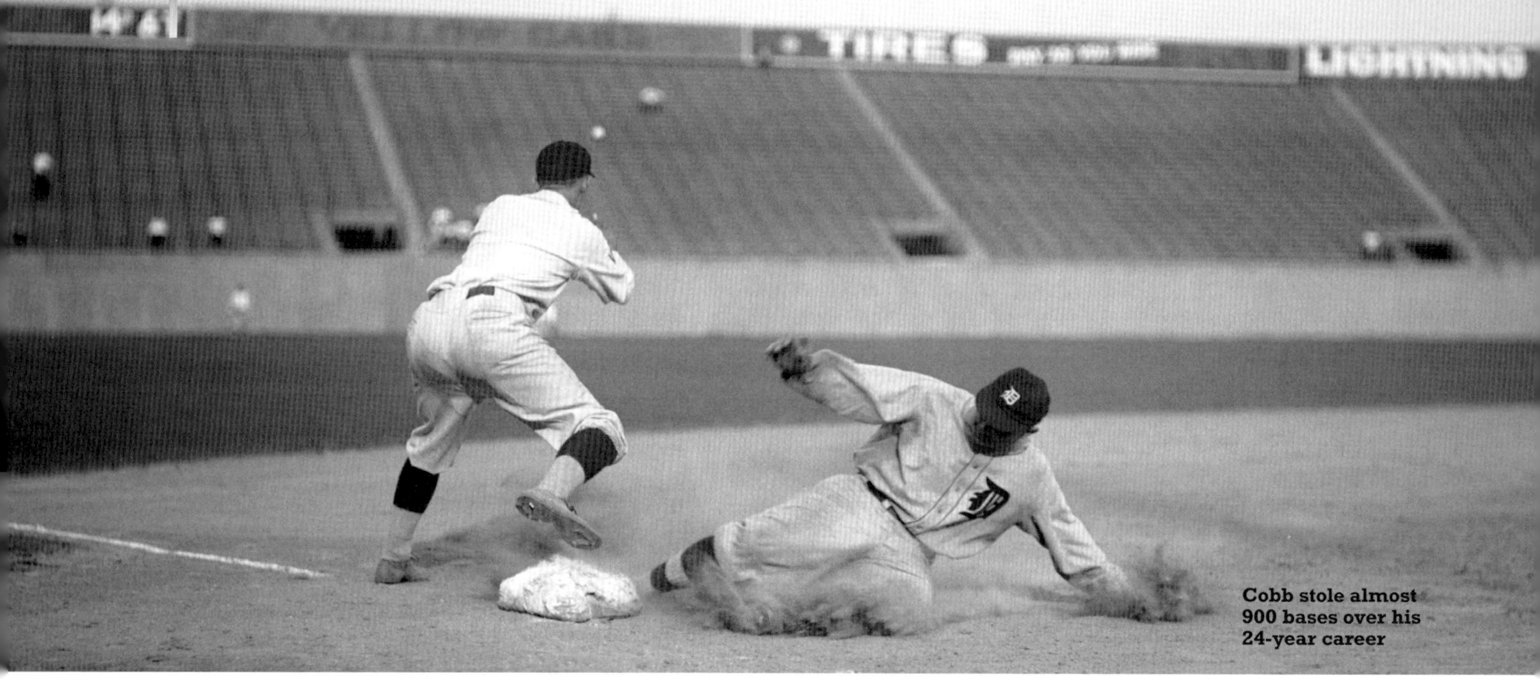

Cobb stole almost 900 bases over his 24-year career

enough to play and record two hits later that day.

Despite his propensity for violence, Cobb's willingness to fight was exaggerated by biographers. One commonly repeated but incorrect story is that Cobb sharpened his spikes to draw blood when he stole bases. Many have tried to slur Cobb by adding a racial component to his violent outbursts. When Cobb and Tigers catcher Charles "Boss" Schmidt got into a training camp fight, Schmidt alleged that he had been defending a Black groundskeeper and his wife who'd been attacked by Cobb. It probably wasn't true. Schmidt had a history of provoking fights with Cobb, and his tall story about coming to the aid of the groundskeeper was likely an excuse to justify his actions.

After the three consecutive losses in the World Series from 1907 to 1909, the Tigers never again won the American League pennant with Cobb on the roster. Nevertheless, Cobb was still one of the best players in the league. In 1910, Cobb duelled with Nap Lajoie of the Cleveland Naps for the batting title. With two games to go, Cobb had a .004 lead, and with the Tigers out of postseason contention, Cobb sat out the final games to preserve his average. During his last two games, Lajoie earned eight hits – six of which were bunt singles – which boosted his average above Cobb's. But the way in which he earned his hits left a sour taste. Lajoie's opponents, the St Louis Browns, had no love for Cobb. The Browns manager ordered his third baseman to retreat to the outfield when Lajoie was at bat, essentially giving him a free single each time he came to the plate.

The messy situation was resolved when Lajoie's final single was ruled as a fielding error due to a wild throw. That dropped Lajoie's average to .384, a shade under Cobb's .385. Usually, the batting champion was awarded a car by the Chalmers Motor Company – but seeing the opportunity for a bit of free publicity, Chalmers decided to give a free car to both Cobb and Lajoie. It was perhaps the right call, because in 1978 a discrepancy was noticed in Cobb's statistical records. Cobb had been incorrectly awarded an extra two hits and his 1910 batting average should have been .383, which would have given Lajoie the batting title.

The following year, Cobb was given the keys to another Chalmers car – this time for winning the MVP award. It was well deserved. Cobb had a career-best .419 batting average. He also led the league in hits (248) and runs batted in (127), both of which were also career-best figures. He had his second-best career total for stolen bases too, including two during an unusual at-bat against the Highlanders. Cobb hit a two-run double, sliding to second base and being called in by the umpire. As the Highlanders argued the umpire's call,

Cobb was a player who fans, opponents and even teammates loved to hate

Cobb's consistency at the plate helped him to 12 batting titles between 1907 and 1919.

Cobb casually strolled to third base, then to home plate, pretending he was listening to the argument. A few metres from safety, he suddenly sprinted to score the game-winning run.

Cobb's consistency at the plate helped him to 12 batting titles between 1907 and 1919 – the only season he missed out was 1916, when Tris Speaker had a .386 average to Cobb's .370. In 1920, however, baseball suddenly emerged from the dead-ball era as Babe Ruth began to bat pitches over the fences. Cobb played on for another nine seasons and became increasingly annoyed with Ruth's power hitting. Cobb also resented the fact that Ruth suddenly overtook him as baseball's most famous name.

In 1925, Cobb tried to beat Ruth at his own game. He announced that he was going to hit home runs, to simply prove that he could. That day, he had six hits in six at-bats: two singles, a double and three home runs. The next day, Cobb hit two more home runs in three hits. Feeling he'd proven his point, Cobb reverted to his old style of play – but no matter how much Cobb complained, baseball had changed for good. It wasn't going to change back to the old ways with him.

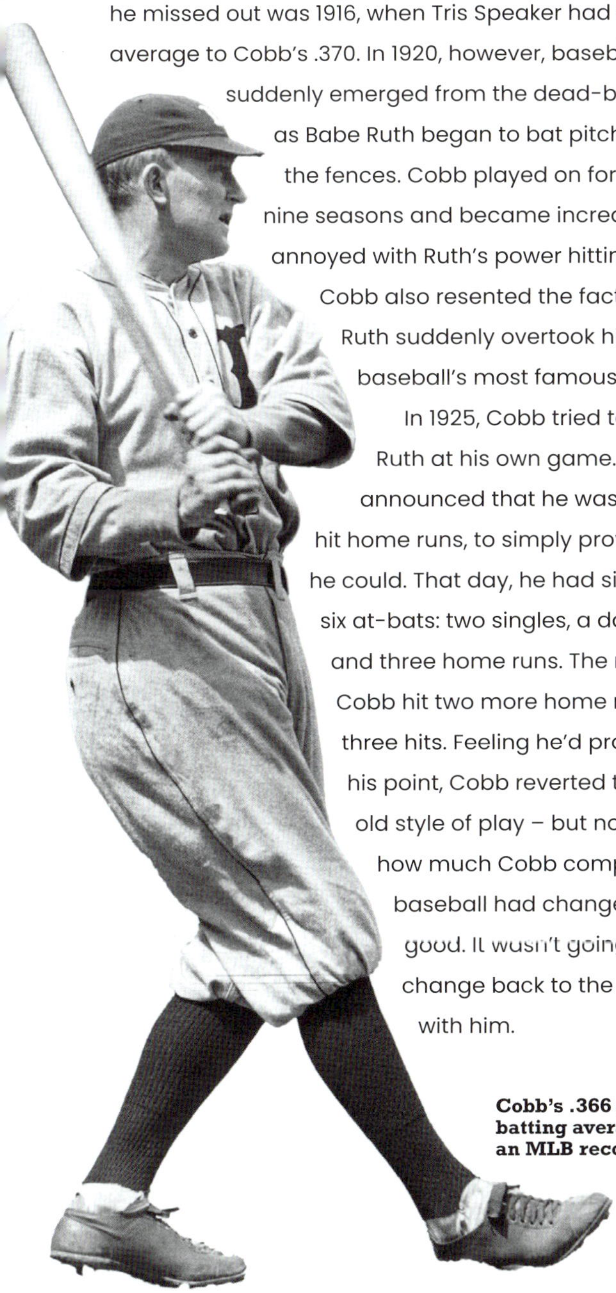

Cobb's .366 career batting average is still an MLB record

Although Cobb wasn't well liked among major league players, his experience made him an obvious choice to manage the Tigers when the job became available in 1921. Under the new boss, the Tigers were still unable to compete for the pennant, and Cobb blamed owner Frank Navin for being unwilling to spend on the best players. Nevertheless, Navin did pay Cobb $32,500 a year – more than half a million today – and had previously made Cobb the highest paid player in baseball.

By the time he retired after two years with the Philadelphia Athletics, Cobb was worth a fortune. Thanks to a sponsorship deal with Coca-Cola, Cobb had 20,000 shares in the company worth $1.78 million. He also accrued $10 million of General Motors stock. Cobb put his money to good use, donating money to build a hospital in his hometown of Royston and a fund to help pay tuition for Georgia students. Cobb's generous philanthropy may clash with the brutal reputation he had on the baseball diamond, but Cobb has often been unfairly maligned in that regard. He was certainly a tough competitor who frequently resorted to violence to settle quarrels, but he wasn't the pantomime villain that many have sought to portray him as. Opponents viewed him with respect, and he gained more votes than Walter Johnson, Christy Mathewson, Honus Wagner and even Babe Ruth to head the inaugural inductees into baseball's Hall of Fame.

GREG MADDUX

Mad Dog

Greg Maddux was a talented prospect from an early age. He was trained by a former MLB scout and learned with his older brother Mike, who was selected in the 1982 MLB draft. But Greg was thought by some scouts to be too slight to be a major league pitcher. How wrong they were.

The Cubs gave Maddux a chance in the 1984 draft, and he debuted two years later as a 17th-inning pinch runner and 18th-inning pitcher in a long loss to the Astros. He made his starting debut five days later and pitched a complete game against the Phillies to secure a win. He soon became the Cubs' ace, winning 18 games in 1988 and 19 games in 1989. He continued to top the charts for the Cubs over the next three years, peaking with a 20-win season in 1992 and picking up his first Cy Young Award.

After seven years in Chicago, Maddux spent the next eleven in Atlanta. He carried on where he left off, winning three Cy Youngs in his first three seasons – the first pitcher to win four consecutive Cy Young Awards. Maddux gained his only championship ring with the legendary 1995 Braves, winning one and losing one in the World Series against the Indians. After Atlanta, he returned to the Cubs for three seasons before seeing out his career on short-term contracts elsewhere.

Maddux's 23-year career saw him gain a reputation as a smart pitcher with supreme control of the strike

During his four Cy Young seasons, Maddux had a 75-29 record with a 1.98 ERA

~ GREG MADDUX ~

Teams: Chicago Cubs (1986-92), Atlanta Braves (1993-03), Chicago Cubs (2004-06), Los Angeles Dodgers (2006), San Diego Padres (2007-08), Los Angeles Dodgers (2008)

Win-Loss: 355-227

Earned Run Average: 3.16

Strikeouts: 3,371

World Series Wins: 1 (1995)

zone and a perfect throwing action. He rarely threw more pitches than were required, meaning there was little wear on his throwing arm, and he only once landed on the 15-day disabled list. It was a remarkably long career for a player who many scouts dismissed as too small and weak for the major leagues.

After seven years in Chicago, Maddux spent the next eleven in Atlanta.

Maddux is eighth on the all-time win list with 355 victories, one more than Roger Clemens

JOE DIMAGGIO

The Yankee Clipper

~ JOE DIMAGGIO ~

Team: New York Yankees (1936-42, 1946-51)

Batting Average: .325

Home Runs: 361

Runs Batted In: 1,537

World Series Wins: 9 (1936, 1937, 1938, 1939, 1941, 1947, 1949, 1950, 1951)

DiMaggio is perhaps the second-most recognisable name in baseball history behind Babe Ruth

The New York Yankees and Boston Red Sox are rivals who've faced each other hundreds of times over the decades – but one particular encounter at Yankee Stadium on 2 July 1941 meant even more than usual. When Joe DiMaggio stepped up for his third at-bat in the bottom of the fifth inning, America held its breath. Pitcher Dick Newsome let the ball go. DiMaggio swung his bat. With a crack, DiMaggio connected and the ball flew over the head of Ted Williams in left field. DiMaggio's home run also allowed Red Rolfe to score and put the Yankees 3-0 ahead – but that wasn't why the crowd erupted in cheers. It was because DiMaggio had broken a supposedly unbreakable record. He'd recorded a hit in 45 consecutive games going back more than a month and a half, and it still stands as one of baseball's most famous all-time highs.

The man who achieved the legendary feat, Joe DiMaggio, was brought up in the North Beach area of San Francisco. He was the son of Italian parents. DiMaggio's father was a fisherman, but his son hated being told to clean his dad's boat. DiMaggio escaped his chores by playing baseball on a playground near his home, and he was taught the principles of the game by his brothers – one of whom, Vince, played for the San Francisco Seals in the Pacific Coast League. When the Seals lacked a shortstop towards the end of the 1932 season, Vince's 15-year-old kid brother was asked to fill in. Joe did enough to retain his spot for the final two games of the season, and by the time the new season rolled around, the old shortstop was told his services were no longer required. Joe DiMaggio was now a fully-fledged baseball pro.

DiMaggio soon displayed a remarkable level of hitting consistency, a feature of his game that would transfer to the majors. He hit safely in 61 consecutive games during his first full season with the Seals – the second-longest streak in minor league history. It drew the attention of major league scouts, many of whom jotted down DiMaggio's name in their notebooks as one to revisit in a couple of years when his body fully matured, but an accident suffered while jumping off a bus soon caused most scouts to cross out DiMaggio's name. He tore the ligaments in his right knee, and the commonly held opinion was that DiMaggio would now lack the speed and dynamic movement needed to

DiMaggio's pace around the bases earned him the nickname the Yankee Clipper in 1939 after a new model of airliner

The DiMaggio brothers all began their careers with the minor league San Francisco Seals

The Other DiMaggios

Although Joe is the one everybody remembers, there were actually three DiMaggio brothers in the major leagues – all of whom played centre field, all of whom were named All-Stars during their careers. Elder brother Vince played ten years in the major leagues for five different teams, making his debut one year after Joe. Younger brother Dom spent his entire career with the Boston Red Sox. And it was Dom who came closest to matching Joe's achievements. Though he never won the World Series, Dom was selected to the All-Star Game seven times.

Dom lacked Joe's raw power (he hit 87 home runs over ten years), but he was a great leadoff hitter with a .383 on-base percentage and .298 batting average. In 1949, he went on a hitting streak of his own. Dom set a Red Sox franchise record with hits in 34 consecutive games. It could have been even higher had Dom not been caught out in his final at-bat in game number 35. In an ironic twist of fate, the centre fielder who caught the ball that ended his streak was none other than his brother Joe.

make it in the majors. Only the New York Yankees were prepared to give DiMaggio's crocked knee the benefit of the doubt, and they bought him from the Seals in a $50,000 and five-player deal. DiMaggio remained in San Francisco for one more year, batting .398 with 34 home runs and 151 runs batted in, before the Yankees summoned him to New York for a closer look.

Thanks to Babe Ruth's power hitting, the Yankees emerged as baseball's premier team in the 1920s. Though always a contender – they won the World Series in 1923, 1927, 1928 and 1932 – DiMaggio's arrival pushed them to an even higher level. He debuted on 3 May 1936 and batted ahead of Lou Gehrig in the order, the position once held by Ruth. DiMaggio immediately set about rewriting the Yankee record books, hitting 29 home runs – the most by a rookie in franchise history. The Yankees won the American League pennant and World Series after a three-year layoff, then repeated in 1937, 1938 and 1939. During that time, DiMaggio was the Yankees' most potent force at the plate. He led the majors in 1937 with 46 home runs and 151 runs scored. In 1939, he batted in 53 runs in August alone, tying the MLB record. His .381 batting average was the best in the league, and he finished first in the MVP voting.

The hitting streak record was broken with a borrowed bat after DiMaggio's usual one was stolen, it was returned a few days later

In 1939, he batted in 53 runs in August alone, tying the MLB record.

After dropping to third place in 1940 – despite DiMaggio topping the league batting average with .352 – the Yankees stormed the American League again in 1941, leaving the second-place Boston Red Sox 17 games back and defeating the Brooklyn Dodgers 4-1 in the World Series. DiMaggio led the majors with 125 runs batted in and earned his second MVP award, but the only stat that interested pundits and fans all year was the record-breaking hitting streak.

At first, the 1941 season looked anything but special. After the Yankees lost to the Cleveland Indians on 14 May, they had a 14-14 record and were 5.5 games back in the American League. DiMaggio's batting slumped to .194 over the previous 20 games. They lost again to the Chicago White Sox on 15 May to push them 6.5 games behind. It was a 13-1 demolition, but at least DiMaggio hit a run-scoring single in the first inning. It was his first hit for three games.

After that, DiMaggio went on the most famous streak in baseball history. The next day, he hit a home run and a triple against the White Sox. He singled in the third game of the series, and he just kept going. On 28 May, the first journalist drew attention to DiMaggio's hitting streak, which had now reached 13 games. He was still a long way off the MLB record of 44 games, set by Willie Keeler with the Baltimore Orioles in 1897, but DiMaggio's hitting was a bright point in what still seemed destined to be a mediocre season.

By the time the Yankees and White Sox met again on 17 June, DiMaggio had tied the franchise record with hits in 29 consecutive games. He broke the record with a single in the seventh inning. One week later, St Louis Browns pitcher Bob Muncrief ignored his manager's orders to walk DiMaggio during his fourth at-bat, giving DiMaggio the opportunity to score an eighth-inning single to increase the streak to 36.

DiMaggio broke the American League record of hits in 41 consecutive games in the second game of a doubleheader against the Washington Senators. He had earlier discovered to his horror that his favourite bat was stolen from the dugout in the interval between the day's two games, but that didn't stop him singling in the seventh inning with a bat borrowed from teammate Tommy Henrich. Two days later, the Yankees had another doubleheader – this time against the Boston Red Sox – and DiMaggio hit in both to tie Keeler's MLB record. The next day, the Red Sox were still in town. Yankee Stadium erupted in the first inning when DiMaggio hit a fly ball to the outfield, but a jumping catch denied him the record. Only in the fifth inning did DiMaggio make history with a home run over the head of Ted Williams in left field.

Despite breaking the record for the longest hitting streak in the major leagues, DiMaggio wasn't done for another 15 days and 12 games. Only on 17 July – two months and two days after the streak began – did DiMaggio finally fail to record a hit. In four at-bats against the Indians, DiMaggio was walked once and had three ground balls that were fielded before he reached first base. Baseball fans let out a collective groan and the intense press coverage that followed DiMaggio's every at-bat for weeks finally came to an end. He'd hit a .408 average during the 56-game streak with 56 runs, 55 runs batted in and 15 home runs. DiMaggio faced four future Hall of Fame pitchers and struck out only five times.

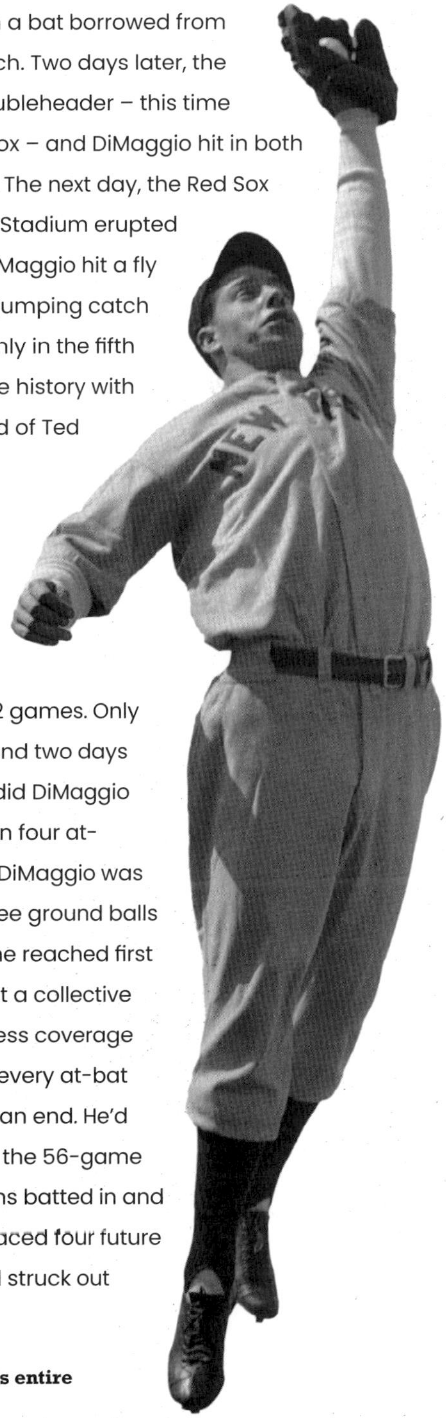

DiMaggio played almost his entire career in centre field

America's First Power Couple

According to Marilyn Monroe's ghostwritten autobiography, she wasn't keen to meet Joe DiMaggio – she assumed he'd be a typical arrogant jock. When they did meet, both were smitten. They eloped in January 1954 and married at San Francisco City Hall. The honeymoon didn't last long. DiMaggio was controlling and abusive. The two fought over Monroe's iconic skirt-blowing scene in *The Seven-Year Itch* and Monroe filed for divorce in October, after only nine months of marriage. In the aftermath, DiMaggio got his life back together.

He stopped drinking alcohol and went to therapy. Monroe, meanwhile, struggled to deal with the impact of world fame when critics panned some of her films and her marriage to playwright Arthur Miller collapsed. DiMaggio got back in touch, securing Monroe's release from a psychiatric clinic, and the two reconciled their friendship. There were rumours that DiMaggio and Monroe might soon remarry, but it never happened. Instead, Monroe was found dead in August 1961 due to a drugs overdose that may have been suicide. A devastated DiMaggio claimed her body and arranged the funeral, then arranged for a half-dozen red roses to be delivered to her crypt three times a week for the next 20 years.

According to his attorney, DiMaggio's final words were 'I'll finally get to see Marilyn'

It wasn't the Yankees' only notable streak of the summer. Between 28 June and 13 July, the New Yorkers embarked on a 14-game winning streak. By the time DiMaggio's 56-game stretch came to an end, the Yankees had vaulted into first place in the American League and had a seven-game cushion over the next best team. At the end of the season – helped by another 16-game hitting streak from DiMaggio – the Yankees increased that lead to 17. DiMaggio's fifth World Series ring was an amazing achievement considering the team's mediocre start to the season.

The Yankees won the American League pennant in 1942 but lost to the St Louis Cardinals in the World Series – the only time DiMaggio lost a postseason series during his career. By then, the USA was embroiled in the Second World War after being attacked at Pearl Harbor. DiMaggio opted to enlist in the US Air Force in February 1943, despite his parents being classified as enemy aliens. Though DiMaggio's mother and father were not detained like thousands of other foreign-born immigrants, they did need to carry a photo ID card at all times and were barred from travelling more than five miles from home without a permit. DiMaggio's father was unable to fish in San Francisco Bay, effectively bringing his livelihood to an end, and his boat was seized to prevent it being used for anti-American espionage. Luckily, DiMaggio's baseball contract gave his family financial stability, and his fame ensured that his war service was comfortable. DiMaggio was a physical training instructor and was not posted overseas. The greatest danger he faced was from fastballs in exhibition baseball games.

DiMaggio returned to New York after he was demobilised in September 1945 and the Yankees resumed their pre-war domination of baseball. They won the World Series in 1947 and DiMaggio collected his third

DiMaggio's fifth World Series ring was an amazing achievement.

DiMaggio had a calm, unflustered batting stance with quick hands that whipped round when a pitcher let go

MVP award. At this point, DiMaggio was easily the most famous player in the sport, but Yankees general manager seriously considered a future without him. The Yankees and Red Sox began negotiations to swap DiMaggio for Ted Williams, another hard-hitting outfielder.

Had the deal been pulled off, it would have been the most stunning transaction since the Red Sox sold Babe Ruth to the Yankees in 1920. Instead, the negotiations collapsed when the two teams couldn't agree terms. If DiMaggio had departed Yankee Stadium, he'd probably have missed out on three more World Series rings. The Yankees won the championship three times in a row from 1949 to 1951, giving DiMaggio nine World Series rings in his 13-year career.

In 1951, the third year of the Yankees' World Series three-peat, DiMaggio felt that his level of play was declining. Though he was named an All-Star – just as he was every year of his MLB career – DiMaggio felt the selection was more due to his reputation rather than an accurate reflection of his current form. He hit only 12 home runs with a batting average of .263. Both were the lowest figures of his career. Rather than begin a slow decline, DiMaggio decided to go out on top. He announced his retirement during the offseason, declaring that aches and pains made baseball less enjoyable to play. He retired with more than 2,200 hits and 1,500 runs batted in – despite losing three years of his prime to the Second World War – and had 361 home runs even though he spent his career in Yankee Stadium, a ballpark that penalised right-handed hitters.

Although his baseball career was over, DiMaggio remained a figure of interest for newspaper reporters. They camped out on his doorstep when he began a relationship with movie star Marilyn Monroe. The power couple married in January 1954 and divorced nine months later. DiMaggio took advantage of his heightened fame to sign lucrative endorsement deals with Mr Coffee (despite rarely drinking coffee himself) and several other brands. He was even referenced in Simon and Garfunkel's song 'Mrs Robinson', leading a new generation of youngsters to ask where Joe DiMaggio had gone without really knowing who he was.

Those who do know DiMaggio as a baseball legend usually remember him for his hitting streak – a record that many think will never be surpassed. As DiMaggio himself said, 'We keep hearing that. It'll never be broken.' But DiMaggio didn't believe in the hype: 'Somebody will come along and break that record.' Even if they do, they'll never knock DiMaggio himself out of baseball lore – he'll always be known as one of the all-time greats.

ROGER CLEMENS

The Rocket

~ ROGER CLEMENS ~

Teams: Boston Red Sox (1984-96), Toronto Blue Jays (1997-98), New York Yankees (1999-2003), Houston Astros (2004-06), New York Yankees (2007)

Win-Loss: 354-184

Earned Run Average: 3.12

Strikeouts: 4,672

World Series Wins: 2 (1999, 2000)

Clemens finished as the MLB ERA leader seven times and had a career 3.12 ERA

Boston Red Sox and New York Yankees fans aren't very fond of each other. It's a rivalry that Babe Ruth had much to do with, after he switched teams and condemned the Red Sox to an 86-year championship drought. But despite a drug-induced question mark hanging over his career, Roger Clemens is one of the few players still idolised by both teams.

Clemens made his debut for the Red Sox in 1984 and quickly took up the number-one position in the pitching rotation. He really announced his arrival in 1986 by striking out 20 batters in a single game against the Seattle Mariners and was named All-Star MVP in that year's contest. Clemens won three Cy Young Awards during his time at Fenway but failed to help the Red Sox

Clemens is a Boston legend for his .634 winning percentage – but that's actually the worst mark of the four teams he pitched for

over their World Series hump. He did achieve a second 20-strikeout game in September 1996 – though few fans realised at the time that it was Clemens' third-to-last game with the franchise. In 1997, he turned down a lucrative contract extension to sign with the Blue Jays. During his two years in Toronto, Clemens won the Cy Young Award twice. In 1999, Clemens moved on in the AL East again – this time to the Yankees.

Finally, Clemens broke his World Series duck. He ended his career with two World Series rings, both gained in New York, in 1999 and 2000. He'd also amassed 354 wins and the third-highest tally of strikeouts in MLB history. Unfortunately, Clemens also picked up allegations of performance-enhancing drug use during his time with the Yankees and three seasons with the Houston Astros. Although Clemens denied the allegations and won his case in court, enough mud stuck that Hall of Fame voters rejected his candidacy during his ten years of eligibility.

He ended his career with two World Series rings, both gained in New York.

TED WILLIAMS

The Kid

Williams studied the science of hitting and wrote a book about the subject after he retired

Ted Williams didn't make the greatest of first impressions at the MLB team where spent his entire career. Williams was a native of California who'd been signed by the Boston Red Sox from the minor league San Diego Padres, and his first major-league spring training camp in Sarasota, Florida necessitated a cross-country railroad trip. The 19-year-old found his way blocked by flooding and he eventually turned up ten days late. The Red Sox equipment manager hailed Williams' belated entrance by announcing loudly, 'The kid has arrived.' For the rest of his life, Williams would be known as The Kid – even when he was a 42-year-old baseball legend who'd also served two stints in the military.

That was all in the future when the Red Sox got their first glimpse of Williams at spring training in 1938. Manager Joe Cronin was impressed with Williams' potential, but Cronin still farmed

~ TED WILLIAMS ~

Team: Boston Red Sox (1939-42, 1946-60)
Batting Average: .344
Home Runs: 521
Runs Batted In: 1,839
World Series Wins: 0

The Red Sox got their first glimpse of Williams at spring training in 1938.

Williams out to the Double-A Minneapolis Millers to hone his game. It was a worthwhile exercise – in Minneapolis, Williams chatted with Rogers Hornsby, a legendary batter and manager whose batting average of .424 in 1924 had not been beaten since. Williams ended up batting .366 with the Millers, helping him to win the American Association batting Triple Crown despite being part of an otherwise lacklustre team.

The following year, the Red Sox hung onto Williams when spring training came to an end. To make room on the roster, they traded four-time All-Star Ben Chapman to the Cleveland Indians. It was a gamble, but one that paid off. Williams went 1-for-4 in his MLB debut against the New York Yankees – a match that featured eleven future Hall of Famers, including Williams himself. By July, he led the league in runs batted in. As the season progressed and he got used to major league pitching, Williams upped his batting average to .327 with 31 home runs. Although there was no official Rookie of the Year title, Babe Ruth was stating the obvious when he declared Williams to be the best debutant of the season.

The following year, a new bullpen in Fenway's right field shortened the distance to the fence. It was nicknamed 'Williamsburg' since most fans thought the bullpen's position was designed to help Williams hit more home runs, and Williams was put in front of slugger Jimmie Foxx in the batting order. Opposing pitchers were caught between a rock and a hard place. If they elected to walk Williams, as they regularly had in his rookie year, they risked Foxx smashing a two-run homer. Even so, Williams' reputation had grown to the extent that many elected to pitch around him and take on the reigning home run champion Foxx instead.

Ahead of the 1941 season, Williams broke a bone in his ankle in spring training that limited him to a pinch-hitting role for the first two weeks of the season. After he returned to full fitness, it still affected his batting stance. However, the injury turned out to be a blessing in disguise. It made Williams put more weight on his back foot when batting, a move which gave him extra control

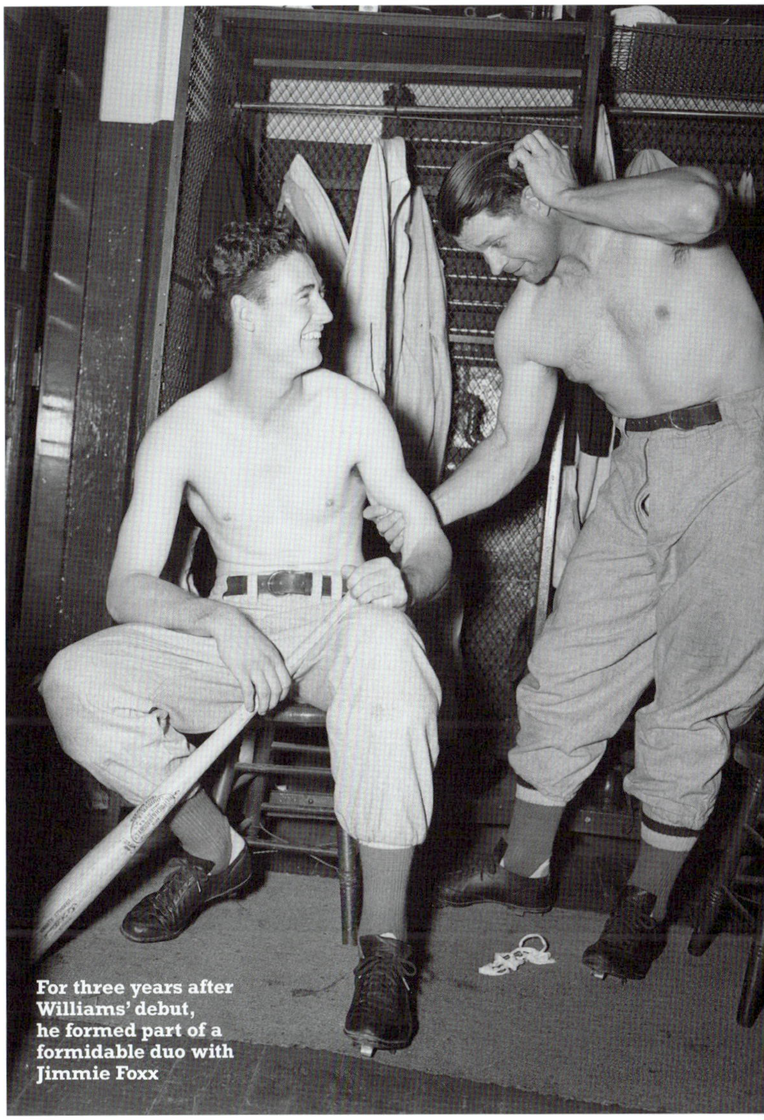

For three years after Williams' debut, he formed part of a formidable duo with Jimmie Foxx

and contributed to a 22-game hitting streak over May and June. He still had power, too. Williams smashed a game-winning home run in extra innings against the Chicago White Sox, a hit that's still considered the longest home run ever hit at Comiskey Park. He also smacked a game-winning three-run homer in the All-Star Game that Williams always remembered as 'the most thrilling hit of my life'.

As the season entered its final weeks, Williams' batting average hovered around .400 – a mark no player had achieved since 1930, and most pundits thought would never be again. After Joe DiMaggio's hitting streak had caught the attention of the baseball world during the summer, Williams' quest for .400 dominated the autumn. By early September, Yankees pitcher Lefty Gomez was booed by his own fans for walking Williams at Yankee Stadium, denying Williams the chance to register a hit. Despite even opposition fans being on his side, the pressure seemed to be getting to Williams. He slipped from .413 in the middle of the September to .39955 before the season-ending doubleheader against the Philadelphia Athletics. Joe Cronin offered Williams the chance to sit out those two games, which would give him a rounded-up batting average of exactly .400. Williams turned him down, saying, 'If I'm going to be a .400 hitter, I want more than my toenails on the line.' His call paid off. He hit six times in eight at-bats over the two games, ending with .406.

Fenway Park was remodelled in 1940, partly to aid Williams' style of hitting

DiMaggio's 56-game hitting streak earned him the MVP award, but Williams' offensive performance was the better over the whole season – and perhaps the best of all time. His batting average remains the last time any major league player breached .400 over a season. He

Three More Hall of Fame Servicemen

~ BOB FELLER ~

Team: Cleveland Indians (1936-41, 1945-56)

Feller won 76 games in three seasons for the Indians, but the day after the Japanese attack on Pearl Harbor, he walked away from a $100,000 contract and enlisted in the Navy. Feller spent 26 months on USS *Alabama*, seeing combat in the Pacific.

~ WARREN SPAHN ~

Teams: Boston/Milwaukee Braves (1942, 1946-64), New York Mets (1965), San Francisco Giants (1965)

Spahn pitched only four games for the Braves before enlisting in the US Army, where he ended up as an engineer at the Battle of the Bulge. He returned to the Braves after he was demobilised and resumed a Hall of Fame career.

~ YOGI BERRA ~

Teams: New York Yankees (1946-63, New York Mets (1965)

Before joining the Yankees and becoming the player with the most World Series rings, Berra volunteered for a special mission to pilot rocket boats that targeted German defences on D-Day. Two months later, he was shot through the hand in the Battle of Normandy.

hit 37 home runs, the most in the American League, and only missed out on the Triple Crown due to DiMaggio batting in five more runs.

Williams was almost as good in 1942. He did get the Triple Crown – .356 batting average, 36 home runs and 137 runs batted in – but missed out on the MVP award again, this time to Joe Gordon. Williams blamed his MVP loss on negative publicity that followed a spat with the draft board. At the start of the season, Williams was called up by the military, but appealed the ruling since he was the sole financial support for his mother. Williams was reclassified and allowed to play ball for another year, but the public and media responded negatively to him supposedly fiddling the system.

There was no way that Williams would get out of military uniform a second time, when he was called up before the 1943 season. However, unlike many of his contemporaries, Williams turned down the chance to spend the war in safety as a physical training instructor based in the USA. Instead, Williams trained as a Marine Corps pilot. When the war ended, Williams was awaiting final orders at Pearl Harbor.

Instead of flying to Japan, Williams returned to Fenway and re-signed with the Red Sox. In 1946, he enjoyed the team's best performance of his career. The Red Sox topped the American League, sealing the pennant with a 1-0 win over the Cleveland Indians – the single run came from Williams' only major league inside-the-park home run. Williams also hit the longest home run ever seen at Fenway against the Detroit Tigers. The spot where it landed in the right-field bleachers is now marked by a lone red seat amid a sea of green. Though the Red Sox lost the World Series in seven against the St Louis Cardinals – perhaps because Williams was hampered with a sore arm after being hit by a late-season pitch – he did win the MVP award for the first time in his career.

The 1946 World Series loss was the only time Williams featured in the postseason, but he continued to be among the league's best players, winning the Triple Crown again in 1947 (one of two players to do it twice) and a second MVP award in 1949. Had Williams improved his batting average by .0002 in 1949, he'd have earned a third Triple Crown too.

Williams' career stats would have been even higher had he not missed most of the 1952 and 1953 seasons after he was recalled by the military for active duty in the Korean War. Although he hadn't flown a plane for eight years, Williams took a refresher course and was soon flying jet fighters over East Asia. During one fraught sortie, Williams limped back to base after anti-aircraft fire damaged his hydraulic and electrical systems and he was forced to make a belly landing. His wingman on that flight was a regular companion during Williams' 39 combat missions: future astronaut John Glenn.

Glenn made history after the Korean War as the first American to orbit the Earth. Williams had already made history on the ballpark before the Korean War. Williams retired from baseball in 1960, hitting a home run at Fenway Park in his last at-bat before wandering to the dugout with barely a backward glance. At the time he hung up his glove, Williams ranked third in all-time home runs. He still holds the highest career batting average of any player in the post-dead-ball era with .3444 and has the best on-base percentage with .482. The Kid who turned up late to his first spring training had turned into one of the greatest batters in baseball history.

Williams was awarded the Air Medal with two Gold Stars for his actions in the Korean War

MICKEY MANTLE

The Commerce Comet

Ever on the search for the next big thing, the New York Yankees sent a scout to Kansas to watch the high schoolers who played for the Baxter Springs Whiz Kids. They'd heard good things about the third baseman and wanted to know whether he was a suitable prospect. He wasn't – but luckily it wasn't a wasted trip. The scout's eyes were drawn to another player who smacked three home runs. He returned a year later to sign Mickey Mantle to a minor league contract.

After two years in the farm system, Mantle was invited to the Yankees' preseason tour and stunned the big-league coaches when he hit two home runs against the USC Trojans. Both travelled at least 500 feet, but Mantle hit one left-handed, one right-handed. Switch hitting would become Mantle's trademark. By batting from both sides of the plate, he could disarm pitchers who relied on control and hitting a particular part of the strike zone against a particular type of player.

The 1951 World Series saw Mantle gain his first World Series triumph, but it also marked his first major injury. While trying to keep out of Joe DiMaggio's way in the field, Mantle twisted his knee and left the field on a

The 1951 World Series saw Mantle gain his first World Series triumph.

One of Mantle's home runs at Tiger Stadium is estimated to have travelled almost 200 metres from the plate

~ MICKEY MANTLE ~

Team: New York Yankees (1951–68)
Batting Average: .298
Hits: 2,415
Home Runs: 536
Runs Batted In: 1,509
World Series Wins: 7 (1951, 1952, 1953, 1956, 1958, 1961, 1962)

stretcher. It was a bad injury – a torn cartilage, possibly a ruptured ACL – and Mantle would play the rest of his career with it never fully healed. Despite his dodgy knee, Mantle racked up 2,401 games over 18 years in the Bronx. He won another six World Series rings, but was never a passenger on the Yankees team. Mantle holds World Series records for the most home runs (18), RBIs (40), extra-base hits (26), runs (42), walks (43) and total bases (123). He was an All-Star in all but two seasons and batted above .300 ten times.

Mantle racked up 2,401 games over 18 years in the Bronx.

Mantle had a higher batting average when hitting right-handed, but hit more home runs when batting left-handed

JACKIE ROBINSON

The Barrier Breaker

Baseball players, fans and pundits always await Opening Day with eager anticipation, keen to see what the new season will bring. When Opening Day 1947 loomed, the excitement was even greater than usual – because six days before the first pitch, the Brooklyn Dodgers called up Jackie Robinson from the minor leagues. For the first time since 1884, Major League Baseball would feature a Black player.

Robinson's path to MLB would have been remarkable even if he hadn't shouldered the burden of being baseball's first Black player in 63 years. He was born to a family of poor sharecroppers in Georgia. Although slavery had come to an end more than 50 years earlier, its effects were still being felt and the Robinsons struggled to eke out a living from the land.

Robinson's father soon left the family home, and one-year-old Jackie moved with his mother and four older siblings to California. There, Robinson was a poor kid in an affluent neighbourhood and risked falling into gang life, but a talent for sport saved him. He represented his high school at football (where he was the quarterback), basketball (where he played guard) and baseball

The Brooklyn Dodgers called up Jackie Robinson from the minor leagues.

Robinson made history as the first player to break the colour barrier, but his performances warrant his status as one of the greatest Dodgers ever regardless of skin colour

~ JACKIE ROBINSON ~

Team: Brooklyn Dodgers (1947-56)
Batting Average: .313
Home Runs: 141
Runs Batted In: 761
World Series Wins: 1 (1955)

(shortstop and catcher) – but it was in track and field where he was expected to excel, since his older brother Mack was a sprinter who won a silver medal at the 1936 Olympic Games. The only runner who was faster than Mack on that day was an athlete who instantly became a figurehead for Black Americans: Jesse Owens. Little did 17-year-old Jackie realize that he also would follow in Owens' footsteps as a Black sporting icon.

Two years after his brother returned from Munich, Jackie graduated high school and remained in education thanks to his prowess in the sporting arena. He broke Mack's junior college national record in the broad jump (standing long jump) and played running back on UCLA's football team, setting a school record for yards per carry. The UCLA roster was the most integrated in college football, but the bar was low – Robinson was one of only three Black players. He also carried on playing baseball, but his .097 hitting average was unremarkable and Robinson regarded baseball as his weakest sport.

When Robinson hit adulthood, the injustices that faced young Black men in the USA began to be driven home. Robinson was arrested in January 1938 after complaining about a Black friend being detained by police, and a suspended sentence would hang over his head for two years. When the Second World War interrupted his studies and Robinson was drafted into the US Army, he applied for admission to the Officer Candidate School. Despite racially neutral guidelines, few Black men were accepted as officer candidates until heavyweight boxing champion Joe Louis kicked up a fuss. Robinson was eventually commissioned as a second lieutenant, but he was arrested and court-martialled by military police in July 1944 after refusing to move to the back of a bus because he was Black. Although Robinson was cleared by an all-white disciplinary panel, the charge meant Robinson did not deploy to Europe with the rest of his unit and he was honourably discharged in November 1944.

Following the war, Robinson became athletic director at Samuel Huston College in Austin, Texas before the Kansas City Monarchs offered him the chance to make a living in his least-favoured sport: baseball. The Monarchs were not a major league franchise. Since 1884, no Black player had been employed by an MLB team. Instead, a network of Negro leagues formed across the country in which all-Black teams played against other all-Black teams, usually in front of all-Black crowds. Robinson was paid $400 a month, but despite the decent wage, he was frustrated by Negro league baseball. The Monarchs were constantly on the road, taking Robinson away from his fiancée. The league was disorganised, with players unaware where they'd be playing from one game to the next. The Negro Leagues were also beholden to gambling interests, and the possibilities of corruption that entailed.

Nevertheless, Robinson's performances caught the eye. In 34 games with the Monarchs, he had the team's best batting average (.375) and on-base percentage (.600). His four home runs were the highest in the team, despite five teammates playing in ten more games. He was an obvious selection for the Negro East-West All-Star Game, where he went hitless but impressed the crowd with his flawless fielding.

It didn't take long for MLB scouts to take note of Robinson's performances with the Monarchs. First, the Boston Red Sox invited him to try out at Fenway, but Robinson was frustrated by the experience. It was little more than a box-ticking exercise so the Red Sox could claim they were not prejudiced against Black players. Although the try-out was held behind closed doors, Robinson could hear racial taunts and epithets directed his way – and the only people they could have come from were Red Sox staff and management.

At least one team had a

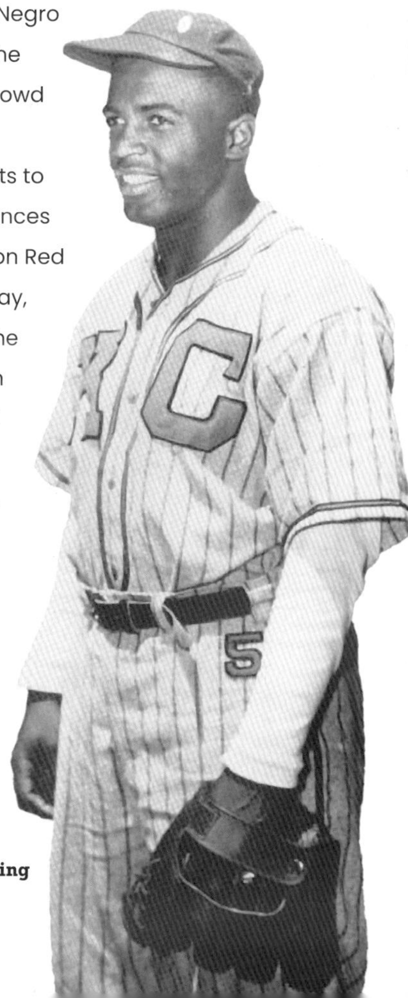

The Negro leagues were a good proving ground for Robinson, but he didn't enjoy the disorganised experience

The Colour Barrier

Baseball's colour line was a tricky and ephemeral act of 20th-century American racial segregation. Although there was no written rule barring Black players from MLB, owners colluded to ignore any talented Black players. The final Black player to pull on a major league uniform was Moses Fleetwood Walker of the Toledo White Stockings, a team that played a single season in the American Association in 1884. Playing briefly alongside him was his brother, Weldy Walker, who spent less than a month with the team. Both had to put up with abuse and harassment.

Cap Anson's Chicago White Stockings refused to play their namesakes from Toledo if the Walker brothers played. After the Toledo White Stockings dropped back to the minor leagues in 1885, no Black player remained on a major league roster, and Black players all but disappeared from the minor leagues too. With such hostility and discrimination, Black entrepreneurs began to form Black-only Negro leagues. The quality of play in the various competitions that came under the Negro league umbrella was high, with a Negro World Series and, from 1971, the inclusion of Negro leaguers in the Baseball Hall of Fame in Cooperstown.

Robinson (number 30, carrying bats) impressed in his season in Montreal and helped win the Junior World Series

Alongside Robinson, Satchel Paige and Josh Gibson were two of the greatest Negro league players of all time

genuine interest: the Brooklyn Dodgers. Club president Branch Rickey recognised that the winds of change were blowing and that Black players were going to end up in MLB, whether baseball authorities liked it or not. Rickey wanted the Dodgers to have first choice from the large and unexploited pool of Black talent, so he sent his scouts to the Negro leagues with orders to identify the best players. They came back with a long list of potential major leaguers, including Robinson's pitching teammate Satchel Paige and Josh Gibson of the Homestead Grays – considered by many to be the best Negro league player of all time.

Rickey wasn't just looking for pure baseball talent. He realised that the first Black player in MLB since 1884 would be put into the spotlight like no player ever had before. Rickey wanted a player who could excel on the field, but also represent all Black Americans off the field. Rickey invited Robinson to Brooklyn and grilled him in a three-hour interview. Worried by Robinson's previous run-ins with authority, Rickey questioned whether Robinson could handle the inevitable abuse without reacting. Robinson nearly ended his chance to play with the Dodgers there and then. He angrily asked if Rickey was 'looking for a Negro who is afraid to fight back'.

Rickey replied that it was quite the opposite. He wanted a player 'who had guts enough *not* to fight back'. In Robinson, he had found the perfect candidate.

Robinson signed with the Dodgers in October 1945 and was immediately reassigned to the Montreal Royals, one of the Dodgers' minor league farm teams – though Royals manager Clay Hopper was upset that his team was used as the testbed for racial integration. The Montreal team had been deliberately chosen to keep Robinson as far from the spotlight as possible – although their newest player's performances ensured he wasn't out of the papers for long. Robinson led the International League with a .349 batting average and .985 fielding percentage. His fielding had improved considerably in spring training after Hopper moved him from shortstop to second base. Robinson helped the Royals to a 100-54 record, 18.5 games ahead of second place, and a spot in the 1946 Junior World Series. There, the Royals defeated the Louisville Colonels. Robinson was named the International League MVP and, perhaps more importantly, won the hearts and minds of Montrealers, including his previously sceptical manager.

Faced with such a talent in their farm system, it was impossible for the Dodgers to put it off any longer.

Robinson's 42 is the only uniform number to be retired across every MLB team

Jackie Robinson Day

Jackie Robinson was inducted into the Baseball Hall of Fame at the first time of asking, in 1962. In a humble speech, he thanked his mother and wife for their support, and Branch Rickey, without whom Robinson would never had a chance to display his talents in MLB. Robinson now had a permanent spot in baseball history at Cooperstown, but MLB soon decided that wasn't enough to mark his phenomenal impact. On 15 April 1997, fifty years to the day since Robinson broke the colour barrier by making his MLB debut, every single MLB team retired the number 42 he played under.

It was an unprecedented honour that ensured Robinson's legacy lived on. Seven years after that, MLB decreed that number 42 would be brought back – but only for one day a year. From 2004 onwards, 15 April marked Jackie Robinson Day. In 2007, Ken Griffey Jr asked for permission to wear number 42 in Robinson's honour. Soon, multiple players repeated the gesture. Eventually, every single player and coach wore 42 in the annual reminder of Robinson's impact on baseball and beyond.

Robinson was ready for the major leagues. Manager Leo Durocher tried his best to dampen the hype by waiting until six days before the 1947 season opener before calling up Robinson to the roster. Since Eddie Stanky was firmly in position at second base, Robinson made his MLB debut at first base. The Ebbets Field crowd was on his side – partly because they knew that Robinson was a player who'd improve their team's chance of winning a World Series, partly because Brooklyn's Black population outnumbered their white brethren in the stands.

On the field of play, as Rickey predicted, Robinson was singled out for rough treatment.

Robinson's fame meant that Black fans turned up to cheer wherever the Dodgers played

The reaction in Brooklyn was largely positive. Around the rest of the country, it was more mixed. Black Americans often abandoned their local allegiances to cheer for Robinson at Dodgers away games, although things were definitely tougher when the team travelled south of the Mason-Dixon Line. Hoteliers and restaurants sometimes tried to deny Robinson admission, but the media spotlight that accompanied the Dodgers meant that physical threats against Robinson were little more than posturing and never taken seriously.

On the field of play, as Rickey predicted, Robinson was singled out for rough treatment. One week after his debut, Philadelphia Phillies manager Ben Chapman hurled racial abuse at Robinson from the dugout, telling him to go back to the cotton fields. The following month, press reports leaked that the St Louis Cardinals were prepared to strike if Robinson was named in the Dodgers team to face them. MLB Commissioner Happy Chandler let it be known that any striking players would be immediately suspended and treated as outcasts. The Cardinals backed down and played the Dodgers, but Robinson ended up with a large gash in his leg after Enos Slaughter spiked him when running for base. Slaughter claimed it was unintentional, but few believed him.

There was unrest in the Dodgers dressing room too. Before the season began, a handful of Dodgers players suggested they'd rather sit out than play alongside a Black man. Team management told them that Robinson was part of the club now, and that they'd happily trade any one of them apart from Robinson. Ultimately, the Dodgers forged a close-knit team, partly thanks to the team rallying around their emerging star when he came up against opponents like Ben Chapman and Enos Slaughter.

Soon, Robinson was not the only Black baseball player and the intense scrutiny over his race moved on. By the end of 1947, four more Black players had played in the major leagues, including Dan Bankhead, who pitched for Robinson's Dodgers. The following year, Robinson's former Kansas City Monarchs teammate Satchel Paige hurled his first ball in the major leagues. Eventually, attention turned away from the colour of Robinson's skin and towards his performances on the field. Though 28 years old, he qualified as a rookie and was named the first ever MLB Rookie of the Year. Robinson had played 151 games and helped the Dodgers to the National League pennant.

By 1949, his third year in MLB, Robinson was good enough to be named National League MVP with a league-leading .342 batting average. That same season saw the first of Robinson's six consecutive All-Star selections. Although he started in the major leagues relatively late in age thanks to the war and racial segregation, Robinson still had a ten-year run in Brooklyn – a period when his team won the National League pennant six times. By 1955, his career was starting to wind down, and he recorded the worst stats of his career. The Dodgers, in contrast, finished 13.5 games ahead of the Milwaukee Braves in the National League and defeated the New York Yankees in the World Series. It was the only World Series ring of Robinson's career, and the only championship the Dodgers won while the team was based in Brooklyn. Robinson hung up his glove at the end of 1956, already a Dodgers and baseball legend.

Few baseball players have a legacy beyond the diamond. Robinson is one of those who did. His contribution to the civil rights movement helped advance the cause of Black Americans both in baseball and wider society, and his life inspired generations of athletes and activists to fight for equality and justice. Martin Luther King Jr described Robinson as 'a legend and a symbol', but Robinson himself summed up his attitude to race relations in a simple way: 'I'm not concerned with your liking or disliking me ... all I ask is that you respect me as a human being.' More than 75 years after his historic MLB debut, there's no doubt that Robinson is now universally respected.

By 1955, the World Series-winning Dodgers included three Black players in their team roster

RICKEY HENDERSON

Man of Steal

Rickey Henderson was born on the back seat of an Oldsmobile as his parents rushed to hospital. As the greatest base stealer in MLB history put it in later life, 'I was already fast. I couldn't wait.' Henderson's unnaturally quick base running helped him steal 1,406 bases in his career. It's a figure far in advance of anybody else – no other player has broken into four figures. Henderson's pace and batting ability (he had a .279 career average and 3,055 hits) meant he was the ideal leadoff hitter – managers could trust him to get onto base and allow those following him in the batting line-up to knock in the runs. But Henderson could hit for power too, and also holds the all-time best mark for leadoff home runs with 81.

Henderson travelled widely in his career, but kept returning to his first club: the Athletics. It was in Oakland that he had his best seasons. In 1980, 1982 and 1983 he stole 100 bases. He was named MVP in 1990 and won his first World Series ring with the Athletics in 1989. His other ring came with the Toronto Blue Jays in 1993. Henderson also amassed ten All-Star selections, one Golden Glove and three Silver Sluggers.

Off the field, Henderson was known for his brash, trash-talking, over-the-top persona. Lots of stories circulate about Henderson's self-confidence in the clubhouse, though many are probably apocryphal. One

In his first season with the New York Yankees, Henderson led the league in runs scored, as well as stolen bases

is undoubtedly true. When Henderson joined the New York Yankees, he was asked about wearing the same uniform as legends like Mickey Mantle and Joe DiMaggio. 'I don't care about them,' Henderson replied. 'I never saw them play. It's Rickey time.' And he was right – in his first season in the Bronx, Henderson became the first person since 1939 to score more runs than games played.

~ RICKEY HENDERSON ~

Teams: Oakland Athletics (1979-84), New York Yankees (1985-89), Oakland Athletics (1989-93), Toronto Blue Jays (1993), Oakland Athletics (1994-95), San Diego Padres (1996-97), Anaheim Angels (1997), Oakland Athletics (1998), New York Mets (1999-2000), Seattle Mariners (2000), San Diego Padres (2001), Boston Red Sox (2002), Los Angeles Dodgers (2003)

Batting Average: .279

Home Runs: 297

Runs Batted In: 1,115

World Series Wins: 2 (1989, 1993)

Henderson travelled widely in his career, but kept returning to his first club: the Athletics.

Henderson was a rare breed: a left-hander thrower and a right-handed batter

Henderson preferred a head-first dive into base since he thought it more important to protect his legs rather than his head

WILLIE MAYS

The Say Hey Kid

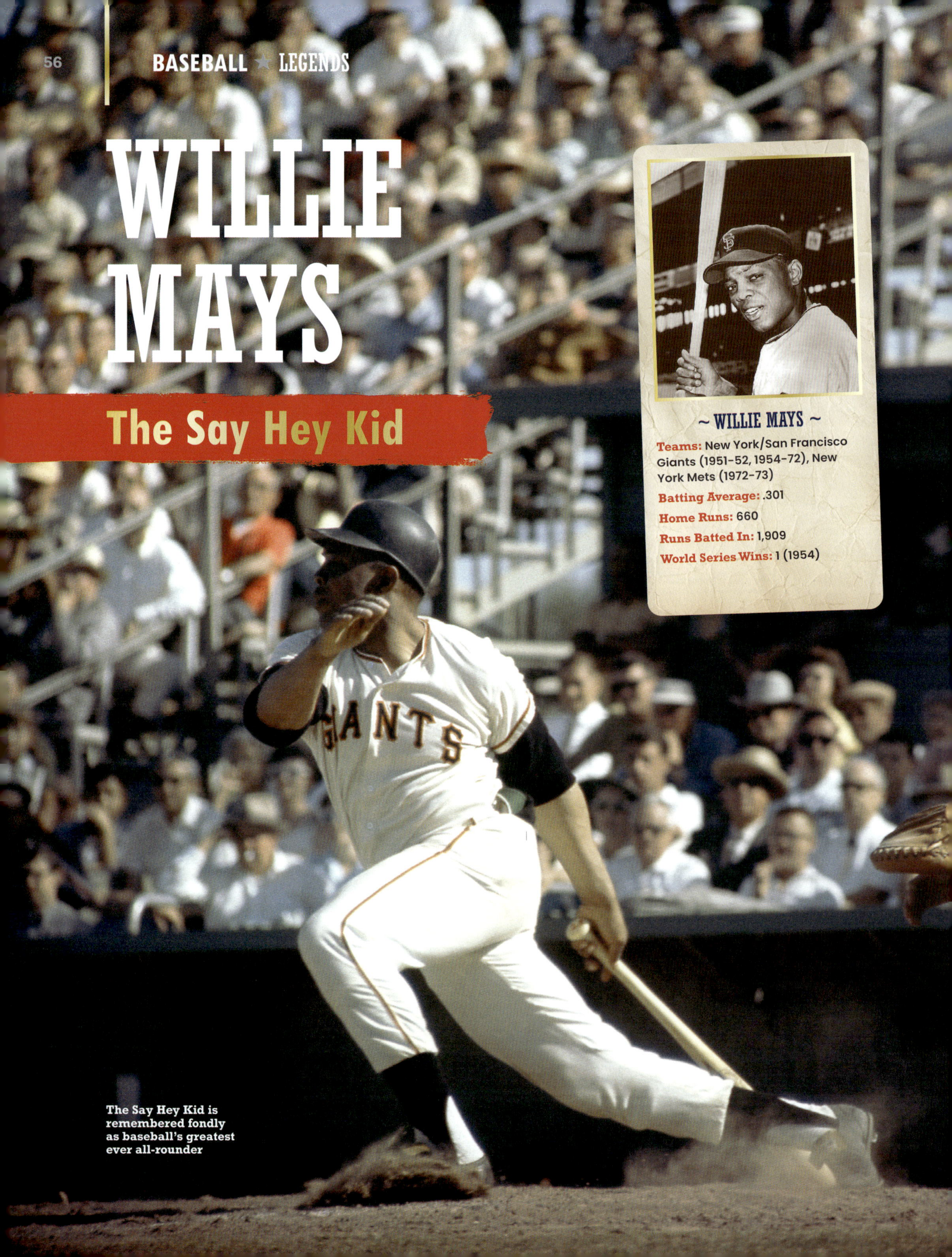

~ WILLIE MAYS ~

Teams: New York/San Francisco Giants (1951-52, 1954-72), New York Mets (1972-73)
Batting Average: .301
Home Runs: 660
Runs Batted In: 1,909
World Series Wins: 1 (1954)

The Say Hey Kid is remembered fondly as baseball's greatest ever all-rounder

The success of Jackie Robinson's first season with the Brooklyn Dodgers led to major league franchises scouting the Negro leagues for talent. MLB bosses plucked the best players from the Black-only leagues, hoping to benefit from the same instant impact that Robinson provided the Dodgers. A few clever operators, however, had their eye on the future too. As well as signing Negro league veterans who'd already refined their game, they also looked for prospects that would boost their team for a decade or more.

In 1948, as Robinson began his second season in Brooklyn, the Dodgers were among the teams whose eyes were caught by a 16-year-old outfielder on the Birmingham Black Barons roster. Willie Mays modelled his game on Joe DiMaggio. His fielding and base running were excellent, and his hitting was a respectable if unspectacular .262. Even though he only played in home matches – a condition placed upon Mays by his school principal – Mays helped the Black Barons advance to the Negro World Series. They lost the series 4-1, but Mays was responsible for the driving in the game-winning run in the Black Barons' only victory.

After Mays graduated high school in the summer of 1950, the Dodgers, Boston Braves and New York Giants offered him a major league contract. The Giants won the battle for his signature, and Mays batted the rest of the 1950 season for a Giants' minor league farm team, the Trenton Giants. Around this time, Mays' charisma and approachability endeared him to fans. They named him the Say Hey Kid due to his habit of giving teammates, fans and even opposing players a cheerful greeting.

Mays began 1951 with the Minneapolis Millers, but he soon proved himself too good for the Triple-A American Association. He batted .477 over the first 35 games of the season, while the Giants spluttered over the first month.

The Dodgers, Boston Braves and New York Giants offered him a major league contract.

Soon, Mays was called to New York to see whether he could help his major league employer. Mays was initially unkeen to answer the summons, claiming he wasn't yet ready, but manager Leo Durocher told Mays to quit fooling around and listen to the guys who paid his wages. He was confident that Mays had all the skills necessary to succeed in the big leagues.

Mays did still require a little fine-tuning. The Polo Grounds had an unusual horseshoe shape, with short left and right fields but a deep centre field. Mays had no hits in his first 12 at-bats, until he smacked a home run against future teammate Warren Spahn over the left field fence. Mays then went 12 at-bats hitless again. Durocher intervened, dropping Mays to eighth in the order to reduce the pressure on him and telling him to stop trying to pull the ball to the short left field – instead, just concentrating on making contact. It worked. Mays got more hits, pushing his batting average to over .300 in the month of June. Mays' improvement at the plate helped the Giants to recover from 13.5 games back in the race for the pennant with the Dodgers. They went 40-18 over the final 58 games of the regular season to end in a tie, and they beat the Dodgers 2-1 in a tiebreaker series to advance to the World Series at Mays' first time of asking.

The Giants lost the postseason contest to the New York Yankees. Mays' boyhood idol, Joe DiMaggio, was named the season's MVP thanks to his astonishing 56-

Four years after Jackie Robinson's debut, the 1951 Giants had three Black sluggers recruited from the Negro leagues

Mays (third from left) played in 24 All-Star Games, tying the MLB record with Stan Musial (left) and Hank Aaron (second left)

game hitting streak. But Mays' average of .274 with 20 home runs and 68 runs batted in was good enough to be named Rookie of the Year and the Giants declared themselves satisfied with their newcomer. Little did they realize that Mays' debut season, impressive though it was, would actually be one of the worst of his career.

The glove used to make 'The Catch' is now on display at the Hall of Fame in Cooperstown

After missing most of the next two years in military uniform thanks to the Korean War draft, Mays fell back into old habits back at the Polo Grounds. He batted .250 over his first 20 games in 1954, leading to Durocher dropping him back in the order. Durocher repeated the same piece of advice he gave Mays at the beginning of his major league career – stop trying to place the ball in left field, just get a hit. Again, it worked. Mays batted .450 with 25 runs batted in over the next 20 games. He earned the first of 24 consecutive All-Star selections over 20 seasons, finished the season with a .345 batting average and 41 home runs, and was named MVP.

The Giants also returned to the World Series to take on the Cleveland Indians. The Indians were heavily favoured, having amassed a 111-43 record to the Giants' 97-57, but the Giants showed their determination in the eighth inning of Game 1. Indians batter Vic Wertz hit a long drive into the Polo Grounds' long centre field – any other ballpark and it would've been a home run – but Mays knew his home ballpark intimately. He set off at a sprint towards the fence, tracking the ball over his shoulder. He knew it was going to be close, looked up at the last moment and took the catch just before the fence. Mays turned and made a great throw to prevent the runners on base advancing, keeping the score tied at 2-2. Mays' play would go down in baseball lore as 'The Catch'. It was regarded as the turning point of the World Series. The Giants won Game 1 in extra innings, then swept the Indians in four to win Mays his only World Series ring.

Although Mays never added a second World Series ring to his collection, he remained one of the league's best players for the rest of his career. He was perhaps the greatest five-tool player in the history of the major leagues: he could hit for average and power, and had great running, fielding and throwing skills.

Mays' play would go down in baseball lore as 'The Catch'.

Mays' ability in the outfield was important in the horseshoe-shaped Polo Grounds. It was even more important when the Giants relocated to San Francisco in 1958. After spending two years sharing with the minor-league San Francisco Seals, the Giants moved to their purpose-built home ground, Candlestick Park, in 1960. Mays and his teammates soon discovered that the new stadium had its own peculiarities, just like the Polo Grounds. At Candlestick Park, the Bay Area's gusty winds made it difficult to predict where high fly balls would land. Mays soon developed a technique to cope. When a batter made contact and the ball went high, he'd count to five before heading after it to allow his eyes to track its flight.

Candlestick Park's unpredictable winds didn't prevent Mays from being awarded a Golden Glove. He won 12 in a row – still an MLB record for an outfielder, but it would have been even more had the award for outstanding fielding been introduced earlier than 1957. Mays' trophy cabinet had other awards in, too. He added a second MVP title in 1965, a season in which he batted .317, led the National League in on-base percentage and had 52 home runs. The span of 11 years between Mays' two MVP awards remains the longest in MLB history, although such was his consistent level of play that he could have won any of the seasons in between – Mays was in the top six in MVP voting for ten of the 11 intervening years. Mays also broke the National League record for home runs in 1966 and led the league in home runs and stolen bases on four occasions.

Perhaps the high point of his time in San Francisco was the race for the National League pennant in 1962. Mays led the team in eight offensive categories, firing the team into a tiebreaker playoff with the Los Angeles Dodgers. The two franchises had moved to new cities since they'd played a similar tie-breaker in 1951, but the result was the same: the Giants won 2-1. Unfortunately, the World Series that followed had the same result too: the Giants were defeated by the New York Yankees.

After 15 years on the West Coast, Mays returned to the East with the New York Mets after he was traded partway through the 1972 season. Although he was no longer the potent force he once was, Mays still made his third and final World Series – a 4-3 loss to the Oakland Athletics. Mays' MLB career had come full circle: a World Series loss with a New York team.

Despite his 1-2 World Series record, Mays is remembered as baseball's greatest all-rounder. Ten times he batted over .300 with 100 runs batted in. He was the first right-hander to hit 600 home runs. He pioneered a new running strategy of attacking the bases, leading the league in stolen bases four times. He was the first National League player to hit 30 home runs and steal 30 bases in the same season, and the first major leaguer to reach 300 home runs and 300 stolen bases. His tally of 12 Golden Gloves remains unmatched for an outfielder. More than anything, Mays was a respected rival and opponent – and considering the era when he played, just after Jackie Robinson broke the colour barrier, that itself was an achievement. Mays was voted into the Hall of Fame in his first season of eligibility with 94.7% of the vote, and as his first MLB manager Leo Durocher put it, 'He lit up a room when he came in. He was a joy to be around.'

SATCHEL PAIGE

The Grandfather

Many presumed the integration of the major leagues came too late for Leroy 'Satchel' Paige. He was regularly acclaimed as the best Black baseball player of all time thanks to his performances on the mound in the Negro leagues, but when 28-year-old Jackie Robinson made his debut for the Brooklyn Dodgers to break the colour line, Paige was already on the wrong side of 40. But that didn't stop Cleveland Indians owner Bill Veeck signing Paige in 1948, hoping to get a good season or two out of the aging star.

Veeck got exactly what he hoped for. Paige made his debut in July 1948, and is still the oldest ever MLB debutant at 42 years and two days. For the next couple of seasons, Paige helped the Indians win the World Series with a 6-1 record and 2.48 ERA – stats that put him in the conversation for Rookie of the Year, despite his advanced age. After Paige made known he thought it inappropriate that he get the honour, the panel gave it to Alvin Dark of the Boston Braves.

Paige was released by the Indians after Veeck sold his interest in the franchise, but his career was still far from over. After Veeck purchased the St Louis Browns, he signed Paige to his new team. Paige became a core starter for the Browns and was selected to the All-Star Game, but was released again when Veeck sold up a second time.

Paige returned to his barnstorming roots and played

~ SATCHEL PAIGE ~

Teams: Cleveland Indians (1948-49), St Louis Browns (1951-53), Kansas City Athletics (1965)

Earned Run Average: 2.70

Strikeouts: 1,438

World Series Wins: 1 (1948)

Paige was restricted to two-thirds of an inning in the 1948 World Series

He was reluctant to hang up his glove, and continued playing well into his fifties.

for Bill Veeck a third time, this time with the minor league Miami Marlins. He was reluctant to hang up his glove, and continued playing well into his fifties. Paige even broke one last age-related record when he made a single MLB appearance for the Kansas City Athletics at the age of 59, as part of a publicity stunt.

Seen here in the dug out, Paige was a showman, often telling his infielders to sit down while he struck out an opposing batter

ROBERTO CLEMENTE

The Great One

At 9:11 p.m. on 31 December 1972, a Douglas DC-7 cargo plane taxied to the runway at Isla Verde Airport in San Juan, Puerto Rico. On board were five people, including 15-time All-Star and former MVP Roberto Clemente. Clemente was foregoing the chance to see in the New Year in style to deliver humanitarian aid to Nicaragua, which had been struck by an earthquake eight days earlier. But he never got there.

Immediately after an unusually long take-off, the pilot radioed air traffic control saying he was making an emergency return. The plane struggled to gain height, and then experienced a critical loss of power. Coming back around to land at the airport was no longer an option. Instead, the plane attempted to ditch in the Atlantic Ocean. It didn't work. The plane broke up as it impacted the waves and all five people on board were killed. The tragic death of one of the leading baseball players of the 1960s stunned the United States. It also plunged Puerto Rico – the country of Clemente's birth – into national mourning.

Clemente was the youngest of seven siblings and stepsiblings. His father was a foreman at a sugar cane

Clemente was the youngest of seven siblings and stepsiblings.

Clemente ended his life with two World Series rings, one MVP award and a .317 batting average

~ ROBERTO CLEMENTE ~

Team: Pittsburgh Pirates (1955–72)
Batting Average: .317
Home Runs: 240
Runs Batted In: 1,305
World Series Wins: 2 (1960, 1971)

In 1998, the Puerto Rico baseball league was renamed in Clemente's honour

plantation, and some of Clemente's earliest memories were of helping his father in the fields at harvest – a busy time of year. The physical work acted as an early form of training, and soon Clemente's sporting prowess was spotted by the adults around him. At 14, he joined a softball team and played shortstop. At high school, he competed in high jump and javelin and was considered a potential Olympian. But it was baseball that Clemente enjoyed more than anything, and at 18 he accepted a professional offer from Cangrejeros de Santurce (Santurce Crabbers) in Puerto Rico's main baseball league. During his two winter seasons with the Crabbers, Clemente progressed from being a benchwarmer to the leadoff hitter with a .288 average.

That was enough to catch the eye of the Brooklyn Dodgers – the team that, seven years earlier, made Jackie Robinson baseball's first Black player in the modern era. The Dodgers didn't expect Clemente – who was also Black – to have the same kind of instant impact, but they did regard him as a prospect who might eventually break into the major leagues.

The Dodgers placed Clemente with the Montreal Royals, a Triple-A affiliate in the International League, the same team that Robinson spent a season with when he first signed with the Dodgers. But whereas Robinson was the focus of intense media interest, Clemente flew under the radar – and the Dodgers hoped it would remain that way. When the Dodgers signed Clemente, his contract included the $5,000 minimum MLB salary and a $10,000 signing bonus. Under MLB regulations, any player with a contract that included a bonus in excess of $4,000 must remain on the major league roster for two full seasons, or else be made available to other teams in the Rule 5 Draft. The rule was designed to prevent a franchise stockpiling talent in minor league affiliates when another MLB team was prepared to give them a chance. By farming Clemente out to Montreal, the Dodgers made it possible for another team to snatch him.

The Dodgers may have asked the Montreal manager Max Macon from playing Clemente too often to ensure he didn't drop into another team's targets. Unfortunately, Macon didn't realise that the Pittsburgh Pirates had an eye on Royals pitcher Joe Black, and he allowed Clemente to work out in batting practice when the scout was watching. Clemente's smooth swing caught the scout's eye, and he rushed back to Pittsburgh with instructions to pursue Clemente. As the scout recalled, 'I knew then he'd be our first draft choice. I told Montreal manager Max Macon to take good care of our boy and see that he didn't get hurt.'

At the end of the season, Clemente returned to Puerto Rico and spent the winter in Santurce, helping the Crabbers win the Puerto Rico league. It was a roster stacked with talent. As well as Clemente, the Crabbers team included future Hall of Famers Willie Mays and Ruben Gómez. It was while he was in Puerto Rico that Clemente discovered he had indeed been selected by the Pirates with the first pick of the Rule 5 Draft. The Dodgers had lost their Puerto Rican prospect. From now on, Clemente was a Pittsburgh player.

The Pirates had no intention of letting Clemente escape in the same way. He remained on their roster and made his debut in the fourth game of the season, going on to appear in 124 of 154 regular season games. The games that he did sit out were due to back pain, the effects of a crash suffered during the winter in Puerto Rico when a drunk driver collided with Clemente's vehicle. The nagging back pain meant that Clemente struggled to swing at certain types of pitches, but he still ended his rookie year with a .255 batting average and impressed with his defensive capabilities in the outfield.

Aside from winning the 1966 MVP Award, Clemente finished in the top ten on seven occasions

Despite performing adequately in the ballpark, Clemente initially found it difficult to settle in his new city. The Pirates and their fanbase weren't as comfortable with Black players as the Dodgers were, having only integrated the year before when second baseman Curt Roberts was called up from the minor leagues. Clemente and Roberts were the target of racist comments from teammates and local media, but the two men formed a close bond and Roberts helped Clemente to settle in Pennsylvania.

After five years in Pittsburgh, Clemente's game

After five years in Pittsburgh, Clemente's game suddenly shifted up a gear in 1960.

suddenly shifted up a gear in 1960. He was named National League Player of the Month after leading the league with a .353 batting average and 25 runs batted in during May. Clemente was named to the All-Star roster, the first of 15 selections over 13 seasons. On 5 August, he made a play that many thought rivalled 'The Catch' by Willie Mays, and the other player involved was Mays himself. Mays slogged the ball into right field and Clemente took chase, just as Mays did in the 1954 World Series. Clemente made the catch to keep the San Francisco Giants scoreless, but when he caught the ball, Clemente crashed hard into the fence. He needed five stitches and a five-game layoff afterwards, but Clemente's vital catch helped the Pirates to a 1-0 win.

By the end of the season, the Pirates were top of the National League. Clemente's first taste of the World Series was a classic matchup in which the Pirates topped the Yankees. Clemente had his first World Series ring. He also had a batting average of .314. The following year, following tweaks to his technique suggested by batting coach George Sisler, Clemente increased his average to a National League-best .351 for his first batting title. Sisler had Clemente use a heavier bat to slow his swing, giving him a fraction more time before the ball connected. Clemente was selected to both All-Star Games that year, earned his first of 12 consecutive Golden Glove awards for prowess in the field, and finished fourth in the MVP voting.

Despite Clemente's ongoing improvement, the Pirates slumped to sixth place in the National League. They remained uncompetitive for the rest of the 1960s, but no blame for their struggles could be laid at Clemente's feet. Instead, he was one of the franchise's few bright spots. Clemente was an All-Star every season of the 1960s apart from 1968, the only year he failed to hit

1960 World Series

When the postseason rolled around in 1960, the Pirates had ambitions to win their first World Series since 1925. In their way stood a colossus: the New York Yankees. In the intervening 35 years since the Pirates last won, the Yankees had collected 17 World Series titles. That alone made them favourites. The series went down to the bottom of the ninth inning of the deciding Game 7. Pirates second baseman Bill Mazeroski was first to bat with the scores tied at 9-9.

He launched the ball into the stands to win the title – the first time the World Series had ever been decided by a walk-off homer. The Yankees were defeated despite outscoring the Pirates 55-27 over the series (their three wins were all blowouts) and despite Yankee second baseman Bobby Richardson being voted MVP (the only time a player on the losing side has won the award). Clemente batted .310 in the series, hitting safely at least once in every game and batting in runs in Games 1 and 5.

The Pirates' win in 1960 prevented Yankees catcher Yogi Berra earning an 11th World Series ring

1972 World Series

There were eerie parallels of 1960 when Clemente's Pirates won the World Series in 1971: the Pirates were underdogs, the series went down to the wire and the Pirates won despite hitting fewer runs than their opponents over all seven games. The Baltimore Orioles were defending champions, had just enjoyed their third consecutive season with more than 100 wins and swept the ALCS. But the formbook went out of the window after the home team won each of the first six encounters.

The Pirates came out of Game 7 with a 2-1 win thanks to spectacular performances on both offence and defence. Pitcher Steve Blass had a four-hit complete game, while Clemente hit home runs in the fourth and eighth innings to ensure the Pirates won the title. Clemente's Game 7 heroics rounded off a brilliant individual series. Over all seven games, he had a .414 batting average (12 hits in 29 at-bats) and performed well in the field to be named World Series MVP. The Pirates won the title despite hitting 23 over seven games to the Orioles' 24.

Clemente was awarded a new car for his World Series MVP award

above .300. In 1964, 1965 and 1967, his batting average was good enough for the National League batting title. In 1966, Clemente hit 23 home runs and batted in 110 runs – both the highest totals of his career – and was awarded the MVP award in a close contest with Sandy Koufax of the Los Angeles Dodgers.

The new decade offered a new start for the often-mediocre Pirates. In 1970, the second season after MLB had reorganised to divisional play, the Pirates finished atop the NL East before losing to the NL West champion Cincinnati Reds in the NLCS. Clemente's .352 batting average was the best of his career (though not good enough to win the title since Rico Carty of the Atlanta Braves had .366). The Pirates repeated as NL East champions in 1971, beat the San Francisco Giants in the NLCS and won the World Series in seven against the Baltimore Orioles.

The Pirates topped the NL East for the third consecutive year in 1972 but lost to the Reds again in the NLCS. At the tail end of the regular season, Clemente hit a double in the fourth inning against the New York Mets to record his 3,000th career hit. The following game, he tied Honus Wagner's franchise record of 2,433 regular games played. Although Clemente sat out the final game of the regular season, everybody expected Clemente to breach 3,000 runs and break Wagner's record early in 1973. Tragically, he'd never get the chance.

During most offseasons, Clemente returned to his native Puerto Rico to compete in its premier baseball league. Aside from his first team, the Cangejeros de Santurce, Clemente also won the title with the Criollos de Caguas and Senadores de San Juan. Clemente's Puerto Rican baseball exploits also led to him travelling across the Caribbean and Latin America to take on international opponents. In October 1972, he managed the Puerto Rico national team in the Amateur World Series in Nicaragua, helping his team to a sixth-place finish. A few weeks later, as Clemente prepared to celebrate Christmas with his wife and three children, Clemente learned of a 6.3-magnitude earthquake that struck the Nicaraguan capital, Managua, and killed 5,000 people.

Clemente was well known for his ability to punish a bad ball from pitchers

Clemente was moved to help the people of a city that he'd visited so recently. He helped raise funds to pay for life-saving equipment and food, but was disappointed to find that the Nicaraguan military had reportedly seized the aid to sell on at a profit. Clemente organised for another planeload of supplies to fly out to Managua on 31 December – but this time, he decided to accompany the flight himself. Clemente thought his public profile would ensure that the military would leave this cargo alone. If they didn't, he was determined to confront the country's leader himself.

On the day of the flight, volunteers loaded the Douglas DC-7's hold, among them MLB pitcher Tom Walker who was also playing winter baseball in Puerto Rico. Walker offered to join Clemente on the trip, but Clemente insisted that Walker stay behind and enjoy his New Year celebrations. Clemente boarded the plane with a pilot, co-pilot and two other passengers, but the plane was only in the air for a minute before it came down in water at the end of the runway.

Investigations would later show that the plane involved had collided with another aircraft on the ground a month earlier, which may have caused unseen damage that caused the crash. It may also have been poorly loaded. Whatever the reason the plane came down, news that Clemente was missing and presumed dead soon flashed around the world.

Clemente was among four people on board whose bodies were never recovered. Friends and family attended a memorial service, though teammate Manny Sanguillén chose to spend the day of the service diving in the water where the plane went down in a vain attempt to find his friend. Three months later, the Hall of Fame voted to waive the usual five-year waiting period after a player retired and inducted Clemente in a special ceremony.

That same year, MLB Commissioner Bowie Kuhn decided to rename the Commissioner's Award in Clemente's honour. Considering that it's given to a player who 'best exemplifies the game of baseball, sportsmanship, community involvement and the individual's contribution to his team,' the Roberto Clemente Award is a fitting memorial to a player who lost his life in a charitable endeavour to help those less well-off than him. It also ensures that new generations of fans will remain aware of Clemente's name, legacy and impact on the world of baseball.

STAN MUSIAL

Stan the Man

~ STAN MUSIAL ~

Team: St Louis Cardinals (1941-44, 1946-63)
Batting Average: .331
Hits: 3,630
Home Runs: 475
Runs Batted In: 1,951
World Series Wins: 3 (1942, 1944, 1946)

Musial was elected to the Hall of Fame at the first time of asking with over 90% of the vote

Pitchers who first encountered Stan Musial were often perplexed by his batting style. Musial turned his back on the mound as though dismissing his opponent. Perhaps he was – because when they let go off the ball, Musial would untwist and connect with the bat. His style was unorthodox, but nobody could deny that it worked. In each of his first 17 seasons in the major leagues, he had a batting average over .300.

Musial won the Rookie of the Year and the World Series in his first full season in St Louis, bringing an end to the Yankees' phenomenal run in the season finale – the Yankees had won eight times with no losses in the World Series since 1927. After winning a second ring in the 1944 World Series, Musial enlisted in the US Navy. There, he served at Pearl Harbor, working on board a ferry launch in the morning and starring in the naval base's eight-team league in the afternoon. He was back in a Cardinals uniform for the 1946 season, when he carried on as though he'd never been away – batting his team to the World Series and winning his third ring.

The Cardinals didn't win the World Series in 1948, but Musial did enjoy his best year. His always-spectacular batting average reached a peak of .376 in 1948 – a season in which Musial also batted in 131 runs. His tally of 39 home runs was one less than Ralph Kiner of the Pirates and Johnny Mize of the Giants – but had Musial been credited with one home run he hit in a rain-abandoned game, he'd have shared the home runs title and earned a batting Triple Crown. Regardless, 1948 was the last of Musial's three MVP awards – the others came in 1943 (.357 and 81 RBI) and 1946 (.365 and 103 RBI).

Though it's difficult to rank players from different eras, that hasn't stopped many statisticians having a go. According to two different formulae, Musial is ranked as the fifth and third best hitter the sport has ever seen.

Musial won the Rookie of the Year and the World Series in his first full season in St Louis.

Musial's back-first batting stance flummoxed many opposing pitchers

HANK AARON

Hammerin' Hank

The residents of Toulminville, a majority-Black suburb of Mobile, Alabama, were familiar with the sight of Herbert Aaron's son playing in the streets. The Aarons had little spare cash, so young Hank picked up what he could to play the game he loved best: baseball. Using bottle tops as balls and sticks as bats, he honed a swing that would be vital to his success he grew up.

Aaron's high school didn't have an organised baseball team, but he won a spot on the Negro league's semi-pro Pritchard Athletics. In 1949, 15-year-old Aaron was asked to try out for the Brooklyn Dodgers, the team that changed the face of baseball when it signed

Hammerin' Hank was given his nickname in his first MLB season

~ HANK AARON ~

Teams: Milwaukee/Atlanta Braves (1954-74), Milwaukee Brewers (1975-76)

Batting Average: .305

Home Runs: 755

Runs Batted In: 2,297

World Series Wins: 1 (1957)

Aaron's hero, Jackie Robinson. Aaron didn't do enough to win a contract, but he did move to bigger teams within the Negro leagues: first the Mobile Black Bears, then out of state with the reigning Negro World Series champions, the Indianapolis Clowns. One incident during his six months with the Clowns stuck with Aaron into later life. While dining with teammates in Washington, DC, Aaron heard plates being smashed in the kitchen. Upon further investigation, it turned out that the waiting staff broke plates after they'd been used by a Black customer, rather than wash them and give them to a white customer. Sadly, it wouldn't be the last time Aaron faced racial prejudice.

In June 1952, Aaron signed with the Milwaukee Braves and was sent to the Eau Claire Bears, a minor league outfit in Wisconsin. Coaches there refined his technique, changing Aaron's cross-handed batting grip (right-handed but with his left hand higher on the bat) into a more conventional one. It helped Aaron become the unanimous choice for Northern League Rookie of the Year. In 1953, he was promoted to the higher-level Jacksonville Braves. The step up was no problem. The Braves won the Southern Atlantic League with Aaron leading the league in hits, runs batted in and batting average among a host of individual stats. As one pundit put it, 'Aaron led the league in everything except hotel accommodations.' However, as one of the Southern Atlantic League's first Black players, Aaron faced regular discrimination across the South. He was often forced to eat and bed down away from his white teammates in segregated restaurants and boarding houses.

Aaron was deemed ready for the major leagues in 1954 spring training. Milwaukee Braves manager Charlie Grimm put Aaron into the starting lineup after left fielder Bobby Thomson broke his ankle sliding into base. The next day, Aaron hit the first of many home runs for the Braves. He appeared in 122 games in his rookie MLB season before Aaron also broke his ankle, bringing his first campaign to a premature end.

When Aaron returned to the lineup, it was with a new number: 44. It would prove to be a lucky omen. Aaron went on to hit exactly 44 home runs in four different seasons. In 1955, Aaron hit 27 home runs at .314 – good enough for his first All-Star selection. In 1956, he improved his average to .328 and won his first batting title.

By 1957, Aaron was part of the MVP debate. His two-run walk-off home run clinched the pennant and sent the Braves into the World Series. There, they met the defending champion New York Yankees, who'd represented the American League in eight of the

Aaron was deemed ready for the major leagues in 1954 spring training.

Aaron's 6,856 total bases remains an MLB record

past ten World Series, winning seven of them. But the Braves – and especially Aaron – weren't overawed by the occasion. Aaron had 11 hits at a .393 average with a triple, three home runs and seven runs batted in. It carried the Braves to a 4-3 series victory, and Aaron only missed out on the World Series MVP award because pitcher Lew Burdette performed at a stellar level, winning each of his three starts with a .67 ERA.

Aaron wasn't to be denied the National League MVP award. During the regular season, he led the league in home runs (44) and runs batted in (132) and had the third-best batting average (.322). When the MVP votes were counted, he beat Stan Musial by 239 points to 230.

1957 was Aaron's finest year, but he continued to play at a high level for more than a decade. He ranked third in the MVP vote in 1958, a season in which the Braves returned to the World Series and faced off against the Yankees for the second year in a row. This time, the Yankees got revenge with their own 4-3 victory, coming back from 1-3 down in the series. Aaron won the batting title in 1959 with a career-best .355, and he continued to be one of the opponents that pitchers feared most.

In the 1965 offseason, the Braves relocated to Atlanta. By this point, Aaron was a 12-year veteran with 398 home runs, and a change in ballpark did not affect his potency at the plate. In 1966, he led the league in home runs and runs batted in, and in 1968, he became the sixth player in MLB history to surpass 500 home runs. One year later, Aaron hit his 537th home run to move past Mickey Mantle to third place on the list. Only Babe Ruth (714) and Willie Mays (587, and still active with the Giants) stood between Aaron and what many regarded as an unbreakable record.

Hank was always on hand to sign autographs for young fans

By the end of the 1960s, Aaron was in his mid-thirties and had been playing in the major leagues for 16 years. Not many people expected him to keep going at the rate required to threaten Ruth's all-time high, but Aaron proved them wrong. He hit 44 home runs in 1969, 38 in 1970 and 47 in 1971. On 10 June 1972, Aaron cracked a grand slam home run against the Philadelphia Phillies. It was the 649th of his career, a tally that overtook Mays for second place in the career home runs list. With that hit, the baseball world began to believe that Aaron really could chase down Ruth's record.

By the end of the 1972 season, Aaron was on 673. He needed another 41 to beat Ruth, and throughout 1973, the media gleefully reported every single home run that flew off Aaron's bat. Sacks of letters arrived at Atlanta Stadium. Many fans expressed their excitement about the home run chase, but not everybody was eager to see Aaron break the record. The Braves employed an extra secretary to sort through the post and remove any

Aaron hit at least 24 home runs every season for an astonishing 18 years

racist hate mail before Aaron saw it.

Even so, Aaron was aware of ill-feeling towards him. He hit home run number 713 in the penultimate game of the season to put him one away from Ruth's record, but failed to register another homer in his final outing. The baseball world would have to wait until the new season for the record to be broken, but Aaron repeatedly expressed his worry that he wouldn't live to play again. He feared a white supremacist would put a bullet in his back rather than allow Aaron to claim the record. Even journalists who wrote about the home run chase received abusive letters for writing about Aaron in a positive way.

Despite his worries, Aaron was ready and raring to go when the 1974 season started. He smacked a home run in his first at-bat of the first game, a road series against the Cincinnati Reds, that tied the record. Management wanted Aaron to break it at Atlanta Stadium, and Aaron duly obliged at the home opener on 8 April. Los Angeles Dodgers pitcher Al Downing threw a ball and Aaron made a good connection. Outfielder Bill Buckner chased it, but the ball just carried over the fence into the Braves bullpen.

Aaron left the Braves at the end of the season but expressed his desire to keep playing. He returned to Milwaukee with the Brewers and played two more years, breaking another of Ruth's records – the all-time RBI total – and was selected in a record 25th All-Star Game (though he only played in 24, a number shared with Willie Mays and Stan Musial). By the time Aaron put down his bat for the final time, he had 755 home runs and 2,297 runs batted in. The RBI record still stands. For many fans, Hammerin' Hank is also the true home run king, having averaged over 32 home runs and 99 runs batted in over a record-breaking 23-year career.

Three More Power Hitters

~ JIMMIE FOXX ~

Teams: Philadelphia Athletics (1925-35), Boston Red Sox (1936-42), Chicago Cubs (1942, 1944), Philadelphia Phillies (1945)

Foxx was the second player to 500 home runs in his career, and still the youngest at 32 years old. The true successor to Babe Ruth, he broke many of the Bambino's records including 12 consecutive seasons with more than 30 home runs.

~ JIM THOME ~

Teams: Cleveland Indians (1991-2002), Philadelphia Phillies (2003-05), Chicago White Sox (2006-09), Los Angeles Dodgers (2009), Minnesota Twins (2010-11), Cleveland Indians (2011), Philadelphia Phillies (2012), Baltimore Orioles (2012)

Much-travelled Thome brought his distinctive brand of batting to many different teams. He based his batting stance on Robert Redford in *The Natural*, a 1984 film about an aging baseball star. It gave Thome a Hollywood-style ability to hit walk-off home runs – his tally of 13 is still an MLB record.

~ MARK McGWIRE ~

Teams: Oakland Athletics (1986-97), St Louis Cardinals (1997-2001)

For three years, McGwire held the single-season record for home runs with 70. He still has the least amount of at-bats to 500 home runs (5,487) and the fewest career at-bats per home run (10.6). But those achievements are tainted by McGwire's admission that he used steroids for most of his career.

LOU GEHRIG

The Iron Horse

Gehrig played well enough that Huggins decided to keep him in the team after Pipp recovered.

Poor old Wally Pipp. The two-time American League home run leader turned up to Yankee Stadium one day in 1925 complaining of a headache. Manager Miller Huggins told him to take two aspirin and have a day off – he'd let Pipp's understudy, a youngster named Lou Gehrig, have a run out in the field. Prior to that day, Gehrig had been limited to occasional

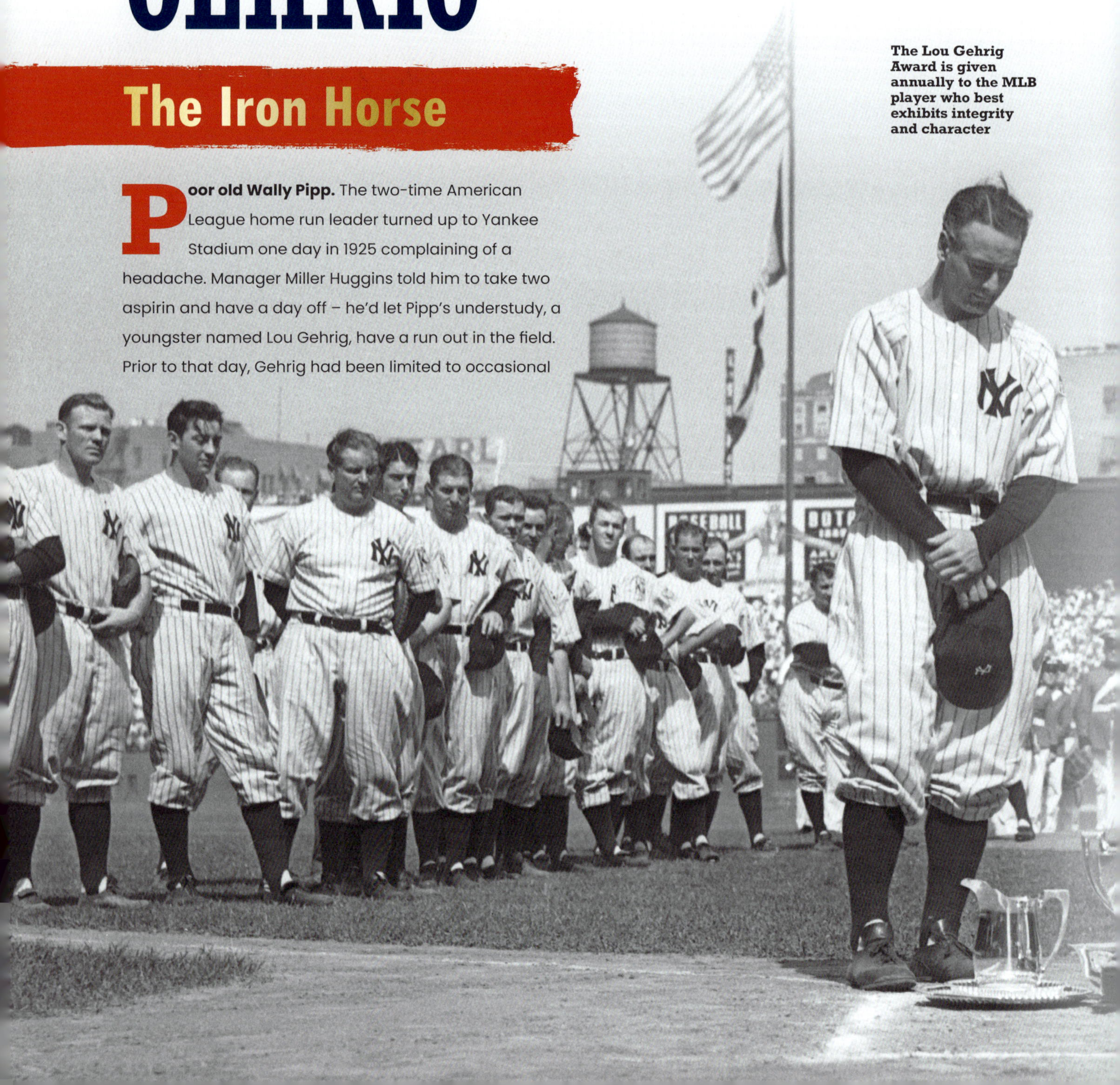

The Lou Gehrig Award is given annually to the MLB player who best exhibits integrity and character

The Iron Horse was so much more than just a regular player.

appearances as a pinch hitter. Not any longer. Gehrig played well enough that Huggins decided to keep him in the team after Pipp recovered, and Gehrig didn't miss a Yankee game for the next 14 years.

The Iron Horse was so much more than just a regular player. He was a seven-time All-Star, six-time World Series winner and two-time MVP. Gehrig followed Babe Ruth – not just in the batting lineup, but in his style of play. Gehrig won the batting Triple Crown in 1934 and had a career .340 batting average. He hit 493 home runs, had 1,995 runs batted in, and retired with the most career grand slams.

Midway through the 1938 season, Gehrig could tell something wasn't quite right. He felt tired and lacked strength. It wasn't enough to pull him from the team until April 1939, when Gehrig recognised his performances didn't warrant inclusion and he Wally Pipped himself, voluntarily taking to the bench. Gehrig continued to suffer a physical decline and was diagnosed with amyotrophic lateral sclerosis – ALS – during the summer. He announced his immediate retirement and the Yankees rushed to declare 4 July 1939 as Lou Gehrig Day with a special commemoration of their popular player. Gehrig was already showing signs of frailty, but he delivered a speech in which he declared himself to be 'the luckiest man on the face of the earth'. He was entered into the Hall of Fame in a special election and the Yankees retired his number four jersey. Gehrig died two years later at the age of 37.

Gehrig was the first player to have his uniform number retired by an MLB team

~ LOU GEHRIG ~

Team: New York Yankees (1923-39)
Batting Average: .340
Hits: 2,721
Home Runs: 493
Runs Batted In: 1,995
World Series Wins: 6 (1927, 1928, 1932, 1936, 1937, 1938)

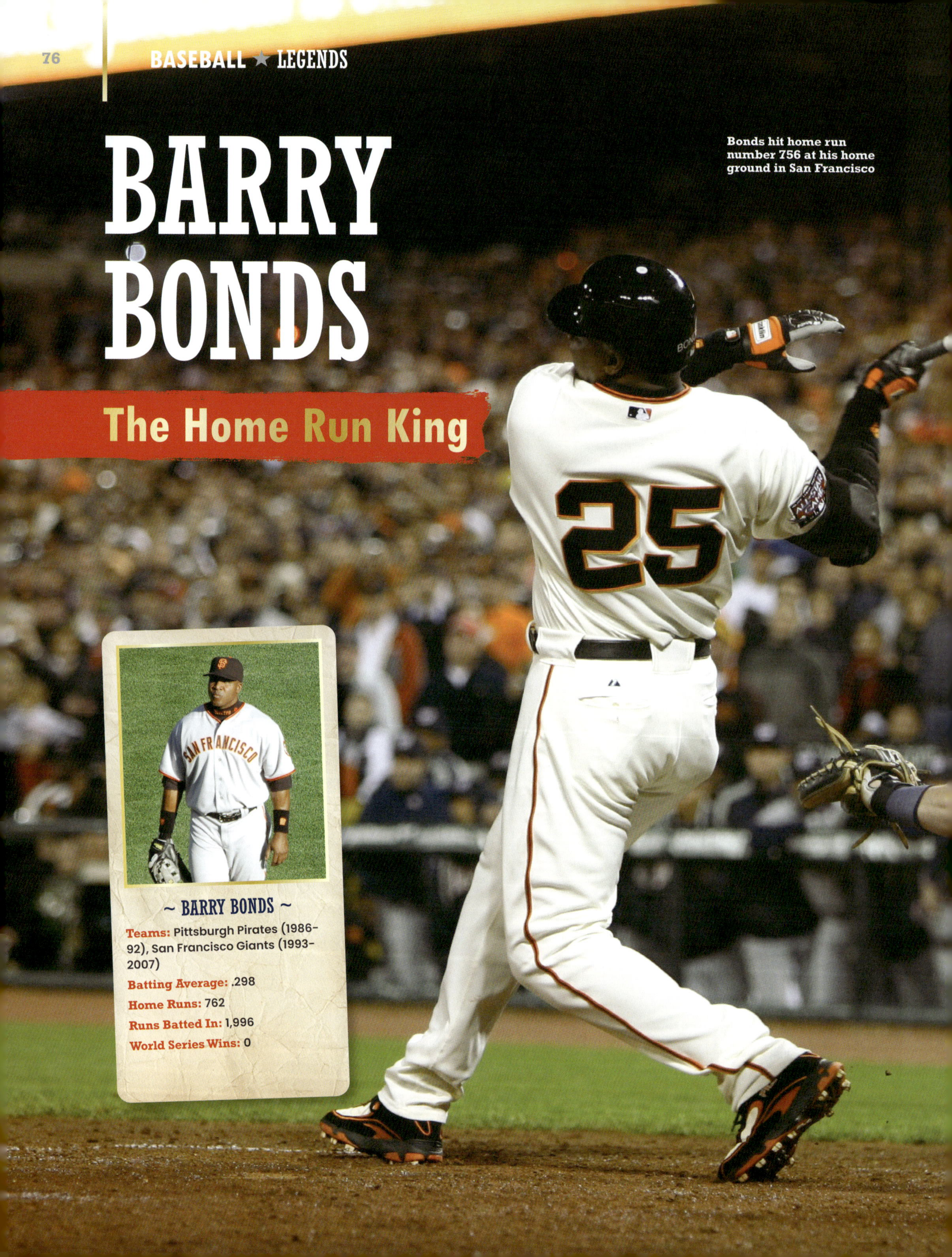

BARRY BONDS

The Home Run King

Bonds hit home run number 756 at his home ground in San Francisco

~ BARRY BONDS ~

Teams: Pittsburgh Pirates (1986-92), San Francisco Giants (1993-2007)

Batting Average: .298

Home Runs: 762

Runs Batted In: 1,996

World Series Wins: 0

On 7 August 2007, the crowd at AT&T Park in San Francisco rippled with anticipation – just as they had every time Barry Bonds had come to the plate for the past few days. Washington Nationals pitcher Mike Bacsik let go a pitch and Bonds swung his bat. A crack signified that he'd connected with the ball, and the crowd erupted as it flew over the centre field fence.

It was home run number 756 of Bonds' career, breaking the record held for 33 years by Hank Aaron. A ten-minute pause ensued during which Aaron delivered a congratulatory message over the big screen and Bonds thanked the crowd over the tannoy. A couple of weeks later, the city of San Francisco honoured their record-breaker with an event in which luminaries including Wayne Gretzky, Michael Jordan and Joe Montana sent their congratulations.

But behind the celebrations and away from San Francisco, many baseball fans were uneasy. The record-setting ball was sold at auction and its new owner donated to the Baseball Hall of Fame, but not before it had a gold asterisk prominently added to it. The message was clear: Bonds may hold the all-time home runs record, but there's an asterisk next to his name in the record books because many believe he got there by cheating.

Bonds broke the record while playing for the San Francisco Giants, a team that his father Bobby played seven seasons with, and whose teammate Willie Mays agreed to be Barry's godfather. Nevertheless, Bonds initially turned down the chance to play for the Giants when they drafted him straight out of high school in 1982. The Giants weren't prepared to go higher than a $70,000 contract, but Bonds insisted he wasn't going lower than $75,000. Instead, he played the long game and took up a scholarship at Arizona State University to refine his game in the college leagues. It worked. Bonds' hitting stats improved each of his three years until he graduated with a degree in criminology, a subject that would come in useful in later life.

In college, Bonds wasn't popular among his teammates. It was a pattern that featured throughout

Though an undoubted talent, Bonds wasn't a popular player among his peers

Bonds broke the record while playing for the San Francisco Giants.

his career. Fellow Arizona State Sun Devils thought that Bonds was rude and self-centred. Despite being the standout player on the team, his teammates voted to suspend Bonds when he broke curfew rather than allow him straight back onto the team without consequences.

Three years after turning down the Giants, Bonds was drafted again, this time by the Pittsburgh Pirates. Thanks to his high-level college play, he jumped from the second round of the draft to the sixth overall pick, and Bonds accepted the Pirates' offer. Yet Pittsburgh wasn't the kind of destination where major league prospects dreamed of playing in the mid-1980s. After winning the World Series in 1979, the Pirates had slumped to the bottom of the NL East. Worse, eleven players were suspended as part of an investigation into recreational drug-taking, and it soon emerged that cocaine use was rife at Three Rivers Stadium. Attendance dropped to less than 10,000 a game, and there was talk that the franchise would soon relocate to Denver.

Amid the Pirates' struggles, Bonds' major league debut was a bright spot. He made his first appearance at the end of May 1986 and soon nailed down a spot as leadoff hitter and centre fielder. Bonds achieved the best National League rookie stats with 16 home runs, 48 runs batted in, 36 stolen bases and 65 walks. The following year, having shifted to left field, Bonds had 25 home runs, 59 runs batted in and 32 stolen bases. He quickly established himself as a key part of the

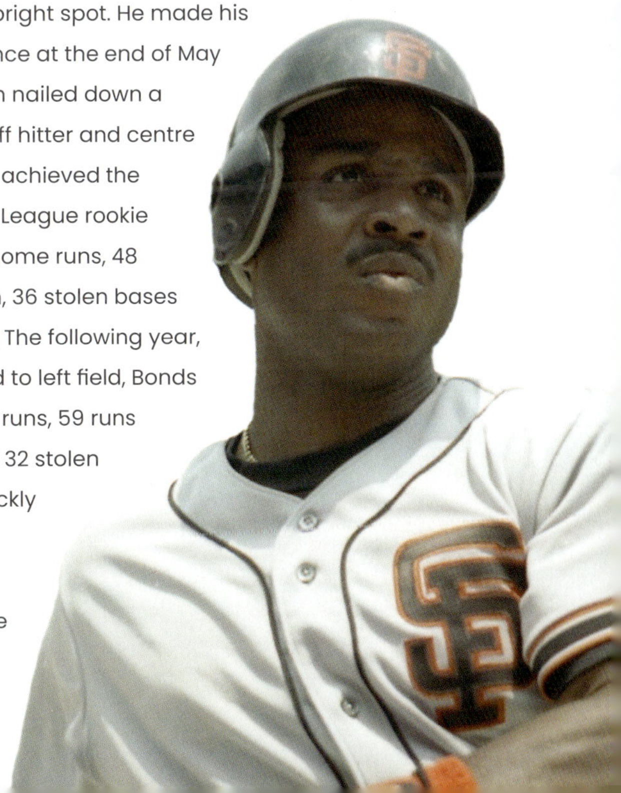

The Alternative Barry Bonds

In 2003, Bonds became the first player to withdraw from the MLB Players Association licensing agreement. For more than 30 years, the Players Association had negotiated the rights for companies to use MLB players' images and likenesses. As baseball's biggest star at the turn of the new millennium, Bonds thought he could do a better job himself. The biggest effect of Bonds' withdrawal was that video game makers were no longer able to use Bonds in their MLB titles – and to fill his spot on the roster, they had to create an imaginary replacement.

The most famous of these was *MVP Baseball's* Jon Dowd, a player whose stats were based on Bonds and was easily the best player in the game thanks to a batter rating of 99 against right-handed pitchers. To avoid a player likeness lawsuit, Dowd was white, used a different uniform number and had the same name as one of the game's producers. He soon became a cult hero. Thanks to *MVP Baseball*, one of the most recognisable players of the 21st century never played a single game in the real-life MLB.

Jon Dowd was a favourite for a generation of video game baseball fans

Pirates attack and helped the team recover to finish second in the NL East in 1988.

The Pirates considered trading Bonds in the offseason that followed a basement finish in 1989, but luckily for them, they didn't. In 1990, Bonds – already a prolific batter – stepped up a gear. He achieved the best stats of his career so far, setting new personal bests for batting average, hits, runs batted in and home runs. For the first time, Bonds joined the 30-30 club for home runs and stolen bases, and he was awarded his first Golden Glove and Silver Slugger. Bonds' power hitting pushed the Pirates from last to first in the NL East, giving Bonds his first taste of the playoffs. The Pirates lost in the NLCS to the eventual World Series champion Cincinnati Reds, but Bonds received a consolation prize when he was named National League MVP.

Bonds finished second in the MVP voting in 1992 and was the subject of trade talks again – this time, he was apparently heading to the Atlanta Braves (who beat the Pirates in the 1992 NCLS) in exchange for three players. The deal fell apart when Braves general manager John Schuerholz opposed it, and for the second time, Bonds responded with an MVP season. He hit 34 home runs (one better than 1990) and had a .311 batting average

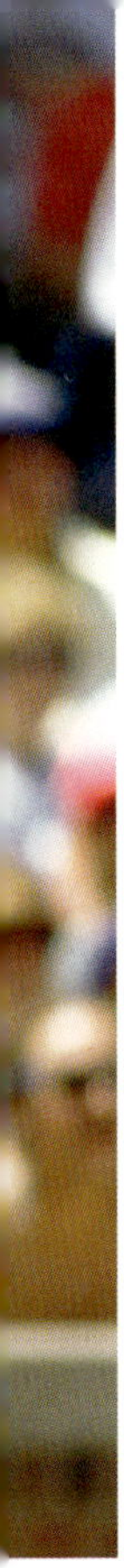

Bonds spent the first seven years of his career in Pittsburgh and picked up two MVP awards

(.010 better than 1990). The Pirates lost the NLCS for the third season in a row, and once again the rumours started that Bonds might be about to leave Pittsburgh.

This time, Bonds really was on his way out. After seven seasons and two MVP awards in a Pittsburgh uniform, Bonds was a free agent. Rather than remain in Pennsylvania, he chose to 'go home' (in his own words) and sign with the San Francisco Giants – the team that he rejected in the draft ten years earlier. Then, Bonds turned down $70,000 a year. Now, he made them pay. Bonds signed a six-year contract that earned him more than $7 million a year. At the time, it was the largest contract in baseball history.

Despite moving to a different team, Bonds retained the NL MVP title in his first season in San Francisco. His .336 batting average and 46 home runs were his best so far by some distance, but in the last year before the playoffs were expanded to include a divisional round, the 103-win Giants were pipped to the NL West title by the 104-win Atlanta Braves and missed out on postseason play.

Throughout the 1990s, Bonds continued to batter major league pitchers out of the park. In his first eight years in San Francisco, he never hit fewer than 33 home runs. In 1996, he became the second player (after Jose Canseco) to 40 home runs and 40 stolen bases in a single season. That provided Bonds some ammunition in the family bragging stakes, since his father Bobby was a single home run away from the 40-40 club in 1973. Also in 1996, Bonds was subject to a then-National League record of 151 walks as pitchers gave up trying to beat him. In 1998, the Arizona Diamondbacks intentionally walked Bonds with the bases loaded, preferring to give up a run rather than allow Bonds the chance to belt a grand slam home run. Three months later, Bonds smacked his 400th career home run to become the first (and still the only) player to have 400 home runs and 400 stolen bases.

Bonds was well on course to claim his spot in the Hall of Fame, and at 34 years old, there was plenty left in the tank. It started to go downhill in 1999. After opening the

The BALCO Scandal

The Bay Area Laboratory Co-operative (BALCO) began operation in 1984 as a vitamin shop and sport supplement supplier. It initially helped athletes to monitor mineral deficiencies through urine and blood testing, but owner Victor Conte began providing his clients with artificial, undetectable performance-enhancing drugs that were concocted by chemist Patrick Arnold. He supplied athletes including former MLB MVP Jason Giambi, Olympic gold medallist Marion Jones and NFL linebacker Bill Romanowski with a range of banned substances.

Among BALCO's products were erythropoietin (EPO), human growth hormone and modafinil. Bonds allegedly used testosterone cream (to trim fat and build muscle without causing a significant rise of testosterone in blood levels) and tetrahydrogestrinone (an orally ingested anabolic steroid to build bigger and powerful muscles). BALCO's shady scheme crumbled when one of Marion Jones' coaches tipped off the US Anti-Doping Agency in 2003. The following year, two investigative journalists obtained an audio tape of Greg Anderson, Bonds' personal trainer, stating that Bonds had used steroids from BALCO. In the aftermath of the scandal, MLB introduced strict new penalties for steroid use and BALCO went out of business – though Victor Conte is still active in the sports nutrition industry after serving a four-month prison sentence.

Bonds was arrested in 2007 by detectives investigating possible perjury and obstruction of justice in the BALCO scandal

Bonds is the only player to have 500 home runs and 500 stolen bases

Bonds was well on course to claim his spot in the Hall of Fame.

season with a .366 batting average and four home runs in April, Bonds suffered a torn biceps tendon and bone spurs in his elbow. When he returned from surgery in June, Bonds struggled to regain his early season form, hitting .248 over the remainder of the season.

It's at this stage of his career that Bonds reached a turning point. In 2000, Bonds stepped up to the plate with a more powerful physique and smacked 49 home runs over the course of the season. The following year, his batting went crazy. He hit 39 home runs by the All-Star break, the most ever. Pitchers began to walk him even more than usual – by the end of the season, he had 177 – and that helped Bonds to a .515 on-base percentage, a number not seen since the days of Mickey Mantle and Ted Williams. On 4 October, Bonds hit a home run to tie the single-season home run record set by Mark McGwire. By the end of the regular season, he'd added another three to finish on 73. Given such a record-breaking season, it's hardly surprising that Bonds was named MVP for the first time in eight years, giving him the fourth MVP title in his career. No player had ever accomplished that feat in MLB history.

Many wondered how Bonds suddenly elevated his already excellent hitting to an even higher level. It's possible it wasn't all natural. Just as Bonds turned up at the plate with bigger muscles and a more powerful swing, his personal trainer – Greg Anderson – had become involved with the Bay Area Laboratory Co-operative (BALCO), a sports laboratory that supplied performance-enhancing drugs to athletes.

Bonds continued to see off major league pitchers.

The ball that Bonds used to break the all-time home run record was marked with an asterisk before it was donated to the Hall of Fame

Though he never troubled the single-season record again, he still managed to hit 45 or 46 home runs in 2002, 2003 and 2004, and won the MVP award each year to take his tally to seven. By that point, however, the BALCO story had broken in the press. Bonds gave testimony to a grand jury in December 2003 that he used a clear substance and a cream given to him by Anderson, but denied knowingly using performance-enhancing drugs. The four defendants in the subsequent BALCO trial, including Anderson, accepted plea deals that did not require them to reveal the athletes they had provided banned substances to. There was no definitive evidence that indicated Bonds' guilt – but as far as many observers were concerned, there was way too much smoke for there not to have been a fire. In the court of public opinion, Bonds was guilty.

Bonds carried on playing for the Giants while the scandal unfolded, and his team's fans continued to view him as a modern-day legend. After an injury-hit 2005, Bonds overtook Babe Ruth's career home run mark in 2006 and started to chase down Hank Aaron's all-time high. He achieved that in August 2007, then allowed his contract to expire at the end of the season and awaited another lucrative free-agent payday.

It never happened. The Giants announced weren't interested in re-signing Bonds, and no other team was prepared to give him a deal either. Bonds spent the next two years waiting for a call that never came, suspecting that he'd been blackballed by MLB owners – though a legal case accusing them of collusion was dismissed in 2015. It left Bonds frustratingly short of 3,000 hits, 2,000 runs batted in and the all-time runs scored record.

MLB owners likely stayed clear of Bonds because he was indicted for perjury and the obstruction of justice relating to his 2003 grand jury testimony in the BALCO investigation. The case took four years to come to court, during which Bonds' former trainer Greg Anderson was jailed for refusing to testify against him. Bonds was found guilty of obstructing justice and sentenced to 30 days of house arrest, 250 days of community service and two years of probation. The punishment was put on hold while he appealed the conviction, and it was successfully overturned in September 2013.

Yet despite legally clearing his name in the courts, Bonds was left in limbo. Six years after his final at-bat, his career was over. He hadn't been found guilty of any doping offenses, but most pundits still couldn't shake the feeling that Bonds' 21st-century achievements were aided by performance-enhancing drugs. During the three years he'd been eligible for the Hall of Fame prior to his appeal, Bonds didn't get more than 36.8% of the vote. Even after his conviction was quashed, Bonds never achieved more than 66.0%. MLB history books will continue to record that Bonds holds the single-season and career home run records alongside a host of other accolades – but like the record-breaking ball in the Hall of Fame, many people will continue to put an asterisk next to Bonds' name.

At the turn of the 21st century, Bonds appeared more muscular than before – a change he claimed was the result of a new diet and exercise regime

WALTER JOHNSON

The Big Train

For right-handers, Johnson let go of the ball in line with third base.

Johnson pitched more than 300 innings every year from 1910 to 1918 yet still had a 21-year career

~ WALTER JOHNSON ~

Team: Washington Senators (1907–27)

Win-Loss: 417–279

Earned Run Average: 2.17

Strikeouts: 3,508

World Series Wins: 1 (1924)

The first time Ty Cobb's Detroit Tigers faced the Senators with Walter Johnson on the mound, the Tigers players fell about laughing. They watched Johnson warming up and eagerly anticipated scoring runs off the tall, skinny sidearm pitcher. Then, Cobb faced Johnson in his first at-bat. He watched as Johnson slowly wound up his pitching action – and then the ball suddenly fizzed through the strike zone quicker than Cobb had ever seen.

For right-handers, Johnson let go of the ball in line with third base. It was difficult to track, yet quicker than the regular straight-overhand delivery used by every other pitcher. Such speed and unorthodox delivery allowed Johnson to compile some impressive statistics. His total of 3,508 strikeouts stood for more than 55 years, despite there being fewer strikeouts recorded in the dead-ball era. He won 417 games, the second-most by any pitcher in MLB history behind Cy Young. He had twelve 20-win seasons, and twice topped 30 wins. No player has scored more than his 110 shutouts.

And he achieved all this in an era when managers didn't protect pitchers from straining their throwing arms. Johnson usually pitched a complete game, most often for a team that offered him little support. The Senators had a losing record in 12 of his 21 seasons, and Johnson's 36 wins in 1913 were 40% of his team's victories over the year. Johnson did earn one World Series win, in a classic 1924 postseason that saw Johnson pitch a crucial stint in relief in the deciding Game 7. That campaign was clearly the best of Johnson's career – he won his second MVP award and third pitching Triple Crown.

Despite his lethal fastball, Johnson had a reputation as a gentle giant, and his popularity among his peers helped him be voted the fifth and final inaugural member of the Hall of Fame in 1936.

Johnson's skinny frame belied his tremendous power

MIKE TROUT

God's Gift

In March 2019, on the opening day of the baseball season, the Los Angeles Angels made an announcement that stunned the sports world. Their star outfielder, Mike Trout, had signed a contract extension that promised to pay him $430 million over the next 12 years. The Angels had gathered all their chips and pushed them into a single pile. The franchise was gambling the next decade on the best player of the 21st century.

Trout was the son of Jeff Trout, a well-regarded second baseman who was selected by the Minnesota Twins in the fifth-round pick of the 1983 draft but failed to make it out of the minor leagues before knee injuries forced his retirement. Young Mike inherited his dad's talent and starred at high school before foregoing the chance to play at East Carolina University to enter the 2009 draft. The Angels selected him with the 25th overall pick and farmed him out to the Arizona Angels in the Arizona League, where Trout hit .360 in 39 games.

Pundits kept their eye on the young prospect, who worked his way up the ladder. Trout was the Topps Minor League Player of the Year in 2010 and starred in

Trout was the son of Jeff Trout, a well-regarded second baseman.

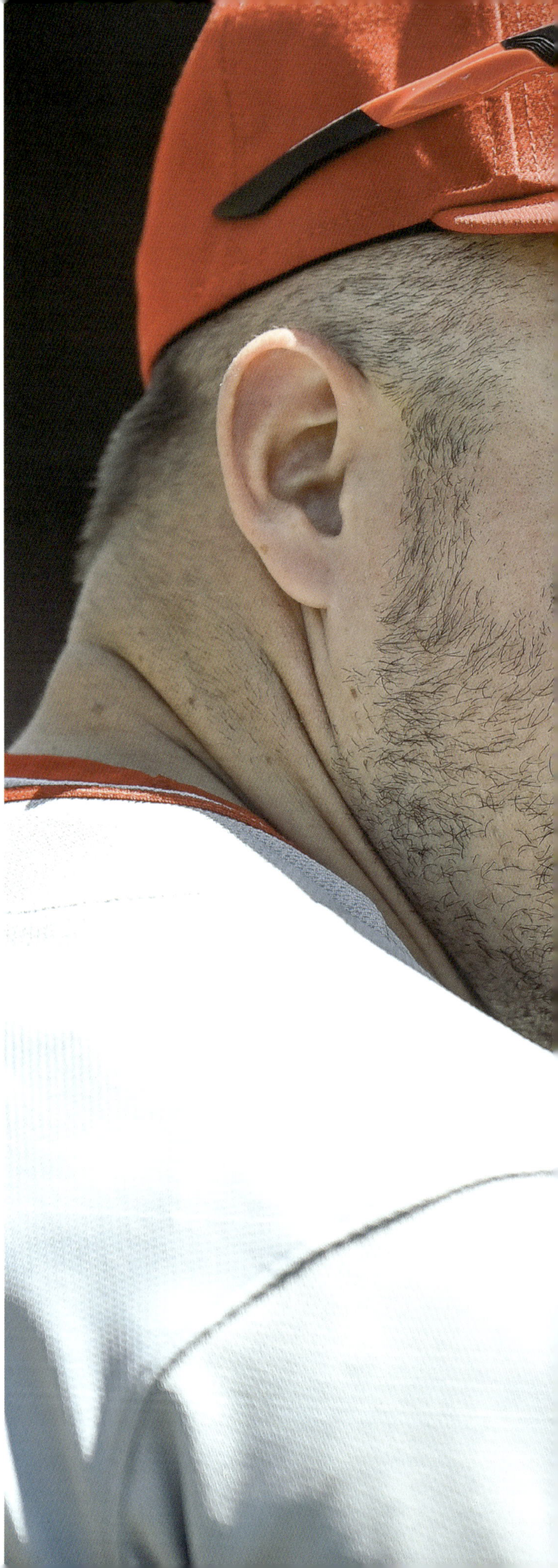

Trout is one of ten players who've won the MVP award three times

~ MIKE TROUT ~

Team: Los Angeles Angels (2011-present)
Batting Average: .299
Home Runs: 378
Runs Batted In: 954
World Series Wins: 0
Stats correct to start of 2025 season

the All-Star Futures Game, getting on base four times and showing off his speed as a base runner. Trout was touted as the number one prospect ahead of 2011. During that year, the Angels used Trout as an injury replacement. He appeared in 40 games and didn't catch the attention of many people beyond a two-homer game against the Seattle Mariners. At the start of 2012, he was back in the farm system – but the Angels recalled him to replace the slumping Bobby Abreu. This time, Trout was ready for the big leagues.

Within five weeks of his 2012 MLB debut, Trout had recorded a four-hit game. He did it again 15 days later, and again eight days after that. Over the course of his rookie season, Trout led the Angels in batting average, runs scored, hits and a host of other categories. Pretty much the only one he didn't claim was home runs – he tied for second place in that category with Albert Pujols. He made magnificent catches in games against the Baltimore Orioles and Chicago White Sox. Trout's 30 home runs and 40 stolen bases made him the first ever rookie in the 30-40 club.

Thanks to his consistently excellent performances, Trout was a four-time Rookie of the Month and the unanimous choice for Rookie of the Year. He was even hyped as a possible MVP. Trout missed out on that award to Miguel Cabrera of the Detroit Tigers, who became the first player to win the American League batting Triple Crown since 1967. The race between Cabrera and Trout proved to be an interesting battle between old and new methods of statistical analysis. Although Cabrera set the league's best marks in batting average, home runs and runs batted in, Trout could boast of a phenomenal 10.9 wins above replacement – a relatively new stat used by analysts to sum up a player's total contribution to his team. To put that in perspective, the next highest WAR was 8.5 (Robinson Canó of the New York Yankees), and Trout was the first position player with a WAR above 10 since 2004.

Trout's impressive performance in his rookie year drew comparisons with his teammate Albert Pujols and the legendary Ted Williams – but in style of play, he more closely resembled Mickey Mantle. Like the Yankee icon, Trout was a quick outfielder with a powerful bat. Between 2012 and 2019, Trout was the most productive batter once statisticians had adjusted for ballpark factors. His .308 average ranked third among 464 qualifying players, his walk rate was fourth, and his isolated power (a statistic that measured a batter's raw power) was fifth.

In June 2013, with shortstop Erick Aybar struggling in the leadoff spot, Trout was moved to the top of the order and immediately contributed two doubles and one run batted in. He scored two runs himself and stole a base. Thanks to performances like that, Trout had the highest win above replacement score in MLB with 9.2, but again lost out to the superior old-school stats of Miguel Cabrera for the MVP award.

Trout finally got his hands on the MVP trophy the next year. He leapfrogged Cabrera courtesy of a stunning All-Star Game and league-leading figures of 111 runs batted in and 115 runs scored. When baseball writers came together to select the American League MVP, Trout was their unanimous choice. He repeated in 2016 – and having finished second again in between, joined Barry Bonds as the only players to have finished in the top two in MVP voting for five successive seasons. As such, it's hardly surprising that Trout was hailed as the best

Trout has a habit of making spectacular catches near the fences

Three More Awesome Rookie Seasons

~ MARK FIDRYCH ~

Team: Detroit Tigers, 1976

Fidrych was an electric pitcher who Tigers fans loved – average attendance at Tiger Stadium was 20,000 higher when he was on the mound. He led the American League with a 2.34 ERA and was chosen to start the All-Star Game.

~ DWIGHT GOODEN ~

Team: New York Mets, 1984

Gooden debuted in the major leagues at just 19 years old courtesy of a fastball and curveball that belied his tender age. He led the majors in strikeouts and opposing batting average during his first year and was an easy choice for Rookie of the Year.

~ AARON JUDGE ~

Team: New York Yankees, 2017

New York slugger Judge hit 52 home runs during his debut season in the Bronx. Though he led the American League in strikeouts, he was also the most-walked batter and ranked second in on-base percentage.

player currently active in the major leagues.

Pitchers complained that Trout had no flaws. Some thought they'd finally uncovered Trout's kryptonite when they realised that he was better at hitting pitches that were low in the strike zone. As soon as they targeted Trout's weakness, he worked at closing the loophole by practising over and over against high fastballs. In 2014, Trout complained that he had the 14th-highest strikeout rate. He worked on that too, lowering his strikeout rate to 26th in 2015, and 59th in 2016. Once again, he identified an Achilles heel and did what was necessary to ensure that opponents couldn't make use of it.

Trout has broken into the top 100 on the all-time home run list

It wasn't just in batting that Trout minutely critiqued his performance. Prior to 2018, Trout ranked 11th out of 17 centre fielders for runs saved. He huddled with his coaches, identified that his flaw was getting into his ready position a fraction too early, and fixed that problem too.

By the start of the 2019 season, the Angels were determined to ensure that their once-in-a-generation talent wasn't lost to another team. At the time, the 12-year, $430 million contract they agreed with Trout was the richest contract in North American sport history, and the second-richest in global sport – only Lionel Messi's 2017 contract with Barcelona was higher. Since then, big-spending Saudi Arabian football clubs have also surpassed Trout's total salary, as has quarterback Patrick Mahomes' contract with the Kansas City Chiefs.

Trout carried on in the same form as before, determined to prove himself worth every dollar. He was named to his eighth consecutive All-Star Game in 2019 and surpassed Barry Bonds as the youngest player to hit 200 home runs and steal 200 bases. At the end of the season, Trout was named MVP for the third time. The Angels now boasted the only two active players in the major leagues with three MVP awards: Trout and Pujols.

Despite their star-studded roster, which included the addition of Japanese pitcher-hitter Shohei Ohtani in 2018, the Angels struggled to prolong their season in the playoffs. Over Trout's first 13 seasons in Anaheim, he only played in the postseason once – a three-game losing sweep against the Kansas City Royals in the 2014 ALDS. Perhaps the Angels suffered a self-inflicted wound by giving Trout such a lucrative contract – it certainly made it difficult to build a complete roster when one player was being paid so heavily.

The gamble of betting the franchise's future on Trout also relied on their star player remaining healthy and maintaining his stellar early-career form as he hit his thirties. In 2021, Trout was 36 games into the season when he tore his calf while jogging the bases. The injury took time to heal, and Trout was eventually shut down for the year. In 2022, Trout missed a month with back spasms, and his 2023 and 2024 seasons were both interrupted by injury.

Now a veteran on the Angels roster, Trout is contracted to the club until 2030. As of the start of the 2025 season, he has a .299 batting average, more than 1,600 hits and more than 950 runs batted in. He's also amassed more than 85 wins above replacement in more than 1,500 games – the leader among active players. Trout currently lays claim to being the 21st-century baseball GOAT, but a World Series ring would allow him to sit more comfortably alongside the legendary players like Ted Williams and Mickey Mantle who he's been compared to.

CY YOUNG

The Cyclone

Young's best season came in 1901 when he won the pitching Triple Crown

~ CY YOUNG ~

Teams: Cleveland Spiders (1890-98), St Louis Perfectos/Cardinals (1899-1900), Boston Americans/Red Sox (1901-08), Cleveland Naps (1909-11), Boston Rustlers (1911)

Win-Loss: 511-315

Earned Run Average: 2.63

Strikeouts: 2,803

World Series Wins: 1 (1903)

Being born and raised on an Ohio farm must have helped build Danton Young's physical frame – it certainly gave him a powerful right arm. He was snapped up by a minor league team in Canton after Young reported that he 'almost tore the boards of the grandstand with my fast ball'. Reporters picked up on the story and nicknamed him Cyclone – later Cy – due to the damage his pitches could cause. A year later, Young signed with the Cleveland Spiders of the National League. For the next nine years, Young's regular catcher put a piece of beefsteak in his glove to try to dull the pain in his hand. By 1892, Young was leading the National League in wins, earned run average and shutouts. In 1895, his Spiders won the Temple Cup (a precursor to the World Series), largely thanks to Young's three wins.

Young moved to St Louis after the Spiders owner bought a second club and shuffled his rosters, but after two years he was poached by the Boston Americans when the American League was declared to have major league status. Here, Young pitched the first ball of the first World Series in 1903. The Americans lost Game 1 but won the series. The following year, Philadelphia Athletics pitcher Rube Waddell restrained the Americans to a one-hit game. He taunted Boston in the press and challenged Young to face him on the mound three days later. Young accepted – and pitched a perfect game. It was even sweeter that Waddell was the last man out.

Young's later years saw him lose pace but develop better control, and he kept winning games. By the end of his career, he had a 511-315 record – a win tally unlikely to be passed. So dominant was Young that a year after his death, MLB created an award presented to the best pitcher each season: the Cy Young Award.

Young signed with the Cleveland Spiders of the National League.

Young holds the current MLB records for wins, innings pitched, complete games pitched and games started

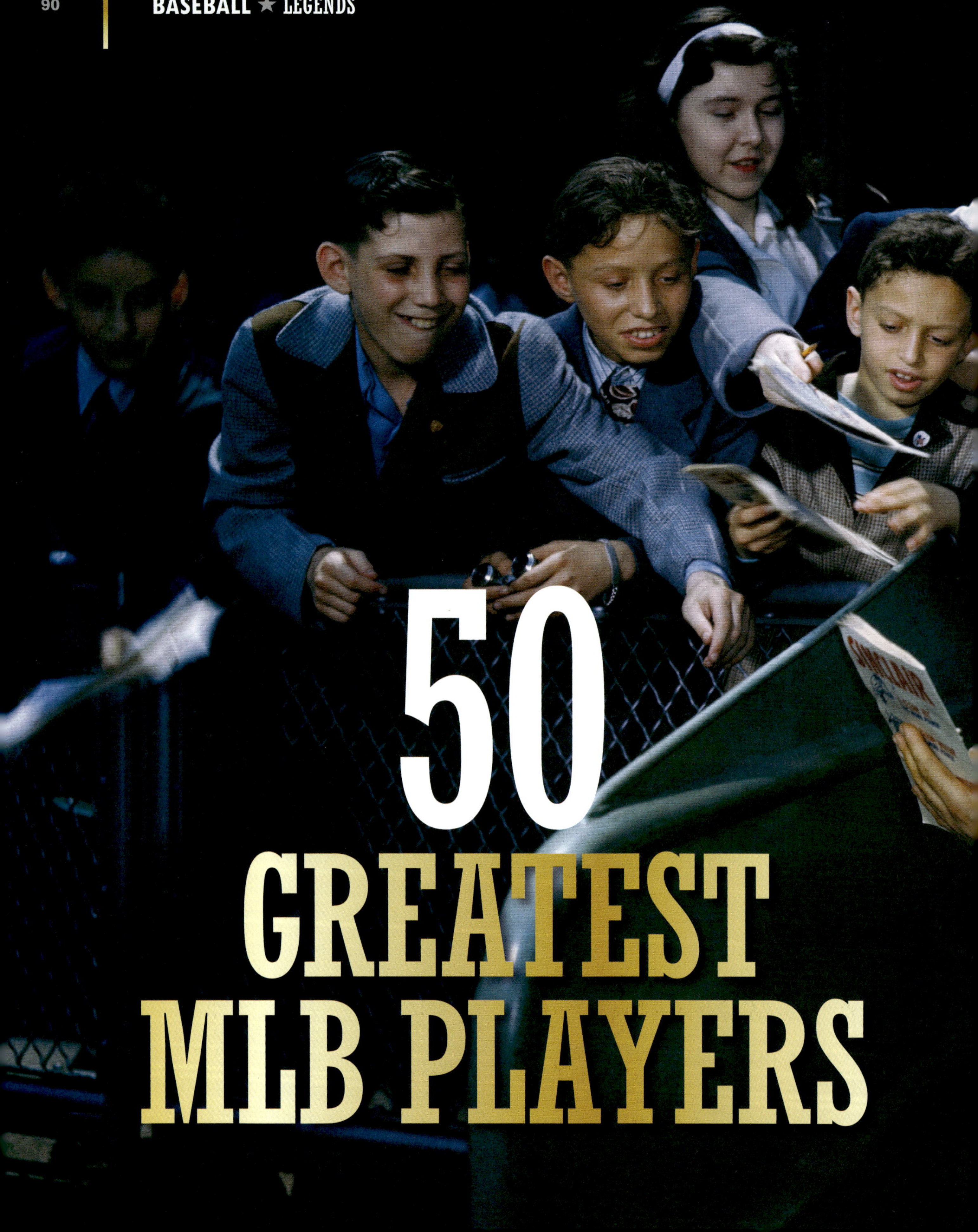

50 GREATEST MLB PLAYERS

Meet the legends who transformed Major League Baseball into one of the world's biggest sporting leagues

When José Godoy made his debut with for the Seattle Mariners on 21 May 2021, it marked a milestone in baseball history: the 20,000th player in Major League Baseball. But not every player enjoys a long and successful career. Less than 300 have been deemed worthy of inclusion in the National Baseball Hall of Fame at Cooperstown, New York. Even among the elite in Cooperstown, a handful of legendary players rise above the rest. This is our attempt to crown the greatest baseball player of all time. From Shoeless Joe to Babe Ruth, here's our guide to the greatest MLB players of all time.

Joe DiMaggio made it into our selection of 50 greatest players – but did he break into the top ten?

JOE JACKSON

50 Shoeless Joe's .356 batting average is the third best in MLB history, but he's been denied a place in the Hall of Fame thanks to the Black Sox Scandal. The 1919 Chicago White Sox were accused of fixing the World Series, and Jackson was one of eight players banned for life – though his level of complicity is disputed.

Teams: Philadelphia Athletics (1908-09), Cleveland Naps/Indians (1910-15), Chicago White Sox (1915-20)

WARREN SPAHN

49 As a child, young Warren wanted to be a hitter. But his father relentlessly drilled him to become a left-handed pitcher, figuring that teams would always be on the lookout for a talented lefty – and it paid off. Spahn ended his career as a 17-time All-Star, and since 1920, no left-handed pitcher has won more games.

Teams: Boston/Milwaukee Braves (1942, 1946-64), New York Mets (1965), San Francisco Giants (1965)

NAP LAJOIE

48 One of early baseball's greatest hitters, Lajoie was a five-time batting champion who won the Triple Crown in 1901. That year, he'd already made headlines when he switched Philadelphia teams to take part in the first season of the new American League. He soon jumped ship again to Cleveland, where the Bronchos were renamed is his honour.

Teams: Philadelphia Phillies (1896-1900), Philadelphia Athletics (1901-02), Cleveland Naps (1902-14), Philadelphia Athletics (1915-16)

CAL RIPKEN JR

47 On 6 September 1995, Cal Ripken Jr broke Lou Gehrig's supposedly unbreakable record for consecutive starts in Major League Baseball. He was ever present for another three years, ending his streak on 2,632 games. But Ripken was more than remarkably durable. He was an All-Star on 19 occasions and the best player on the Orioles' 1983 championship team.

Team: Baltimore Orioles (1981-2001)

TONY GWYNN

46 Another player with extraordinary longevity whose career almost entirely overlapped Cal Ripken Jr, Gwynn put the relatively new Padres franchise on the map. He blasted them to their only National League titles in 1984 and 1988, and in 1994 achieved a .394 hitting percentage. Gwynn was a top defender too with five Golden Glove awards.

Team: **San Diego Padres (1982-2001)**

EDDIE COLLINS

45 Only ten players have hit the ball more times than Eddie Collins in baseball – he safely made contact on 3,315 occasions. But Collins was not a power hitter, and he ended his career with only 47 home runs. Instead, Collins was a supreme leadoff batter with the ability to get on base able to get on base like no other.

Teams: **Philadelphia Athletics (1906-14), Chicago White Sox (1915-26), Philadelphia Athletics (1927-30)**

WADE BOGGS

44 Boggs was a familiar face in the AL East – he spent his entire career in that one division, splitting his time between three teams. He was a five-time American League batting champion, 12-time All-Star, and he finally won a championship during his final All-Star campaign before joining the Devil Rays for their inaugural season.

Teams: **Boston Red Sox (1982-92), New York Yankees (1993-97), Tampa Bay Devil Rays (1998-99)**

GEORGE BRETT

43 One of only five players with at least 300 home runs, 3,000 hits and a .300 career batting average, Brett is also remembered for powering the Royals to their first championship title in 1985. He was named MVP in 1980 and remains the only player to have won a batting title in three different decades.

Team: **Kansas City Royals (1973-93)**

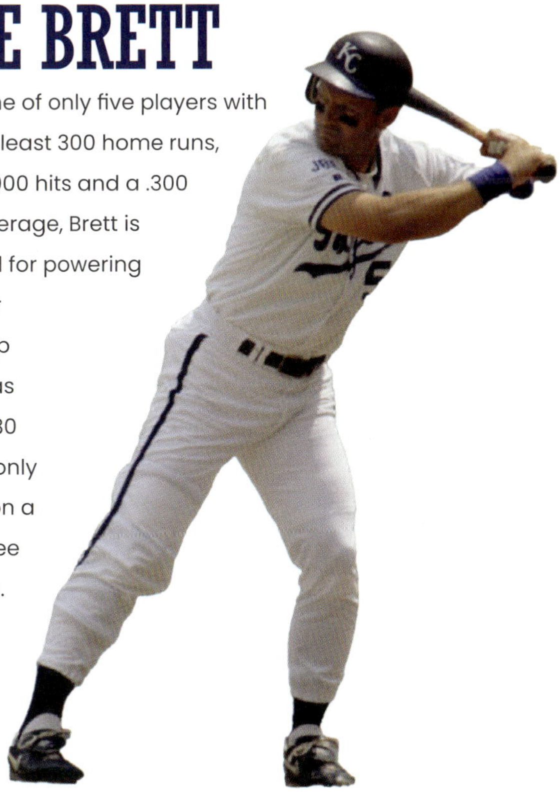

ICHIRO SUZUKI

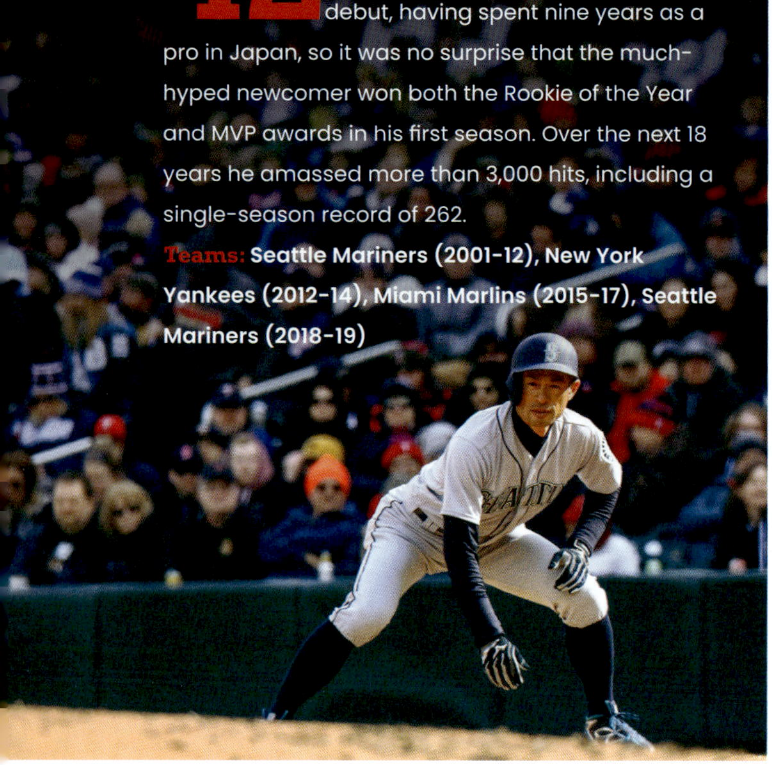

42 Suzuki was already an experienced 27-year-old when he made his MLB debut, having spent nine years as a pro in Japan, so it was no surprise that the much-hyped newcomer won both the Rookie of the Year and MVP awards in his first season. Over the next 18 years he amassed more than 3,000 hits, including a single-season record of 262.

Teams: **Seattle Mariners (2001-12), New York Yankees (2012-14), Miami Marlins (2015-17), Seattle Mariners (2018-19)**

SATCHEL PAIGE

40 After the colour barrier was broken and black players were admitted to the league, Paige became MLB's oldest debutant at the age of 42 – and he pitched one final game for the Royals to become the league's oldest-ever player at 59. Joe DiMaggio named him the best and fastest pitcher he ever faced.

Teams: **Cleveland Indians (1948-49), St Louis Browns (1951-53), Kansas City Athletics (1965)**

JOE MORGAN

41 The Astros traded second baseman Morgan to Cincinnati in 1972, thinking he was a clubhouse troublemaker destined to flame out. How wrong they were. Morgan was an MVP contender for five straight seasons after joining the Reds – he won two of them, the same two years that the Reds claimed the World Series.

Teams: **Houston Colt .45s/Astros (1963-71), Cincinnati Reds (1972-79), Houston Astros (1980), San Francisco Giants (1981-82), Philadelphia Phillies (1983), Oakland Athletics (1984)**

NOLAN RYAN

39 A seriously fast pitcher who frequently hit triple digits on the radar gun with his fastball, Ryan also had a great curveball that tricked batters who prepared only for the Ryan Express. Those two weapons combined to set an all-time record of 5,714 strikeouts. Ryan was also exceptionally durable, good enough to be picked as an All-Star 23 years after his debut.

Teams: **New York Mets (1966, 1968-71), California Angels (1972–1979), Houston Astros (1980–1988), Texas Rangers (1989–1993)**

YOGI BERRA

38

Berra earns a place on this list due to winning more World Series than any other player – ten in all – during a 19-year career. Away from the championship series, Berra won the MVP award three times, was selected as an All-Star 18 times, and is likely the best catcher in the history of baseball.

Teams: **New York Yankees (1946-63), New York Mets (1965)**

JIMMIE FOXX

37

When three-time MVP Foxx retired, only Babe Ruth had hit more home runs. Foxx hit more than 30 in 12 consecutive seasons, including 58 in 1932. He was also a skilled base hitter who won the batting Triple Crown, but it was power hitting that his fans flocked to see. According to Lefty Gomez, 'Even his hair had muscles.'

Teams: **Philadelphia Athletics (1925-35), Boston Red Sox (1936-42), Chicago Cubs (1942, 1944), Philadelphia Phillies (1945)**

BOB GIBSON

36

A long-term ace on the Cardinals' pitching mound, Gibson's career reached a peak in 1968 when he posted a 1.12 ERA with 23 shutouts. Over a three-month stretch he started 18 games, completed 17 of them without needing a relief pitcher, and won 16. He was also one of baseball's first Mr Octobers, ending his career 7-2 in World Series starts.

Team: **St Louis Cardinals (1959-75)**

PETE ROSE

35

Thanks to his prowess in switch-hitting – batting both right- and left-handed, a skill that helped him against a variety of pitchers – Rose is the all-time MLB leader in hits (4,256) and singles (3,215). Over a long career (he also holds the MLB records for games played and at-bats), Rose won three World Series, three batting titles, one MVP award and had 17 All-Star appearances – so it's amazing that Rose has never been elected to the Hall of Fame. That's due to him being permanently banned from baseball due to gambling on MLB games, including those involving his own team when Rose was the Reds manager. Despite his flaws, Rose remains one of the greatest hitters ever.

Teams: **Cincinnati Reds (1963-78), Philadelphia Phillies (1979-83), Montreal Expos (1984), Cincinnati Reds (1984-86)**

MARIANO RIVERA

34 In 1997, after his manager switched him from the starting rotation to a reliever, Rivera discovered how to throw a cut fastball – one that moved towards that batter during its flight. It made Rivera the best closer in MLB history. He used his new pitch over and over again, ending up with MLB records in games saved (652) and games closed (952). His ERA was lower than 2.00 in 11 seasons, and his career postseason ERA was a stunning 0.70 over 141 innings – a figure that helped Rivera and the Yankees to five World Series titles. In 2019, his first season of eligibility, Rivera became the first player chosen to the Hall of Fame by every single elector.

Team: **New York Yankees (1995-2013)**

SANDY KOUFAX

33 Koufax went straight into the major leagues, missing out on a minor league apprenticeship, and it showed during the first half of his career – he nearly quit baseball in 1960 due to his inconsistency on the mound. But after he gained proper control, his now-reliable curveball became one of the best weapons ever seen in the

major leagues. From 1961, Koufax earned seven All-Star selections, was the unanimous choice for the Cy Young Award on three occasions, won the pitching Triple Crown three times and was a two-time World Series MVP. When he retired abruptly in 1966 due to arthritis in his elbow, Koufax had more strikeouts than innings pitched.

Team: **Brooklyn/Los Angeles Dodgers (1955-66)**

TRIS SPEAKER

32 Around the same time that Babe Ruth's power hitting changed baseball forever, Speaker was a master of the old version of the game where the ball mostly stayed inside the park. The three-time World Series champion only hit 117 home runs over his 22-year career, but his batting average of .345 is among the top ten of all time, and his 792 doubles are an MLB record. But the greatest centre fielder in the history of the game didn't just add to his team's score, he also prevented the opposition from scoring. As an outfielder he stood close to the diamond, leading to record numbers of assists, double plays and unassisted double plays.

Teams: **Boston Americans/Red Sox (1907-15), Cleveland Indians (1916-26), Washington Senators (1927), Philadelphia Athletics (1928)**

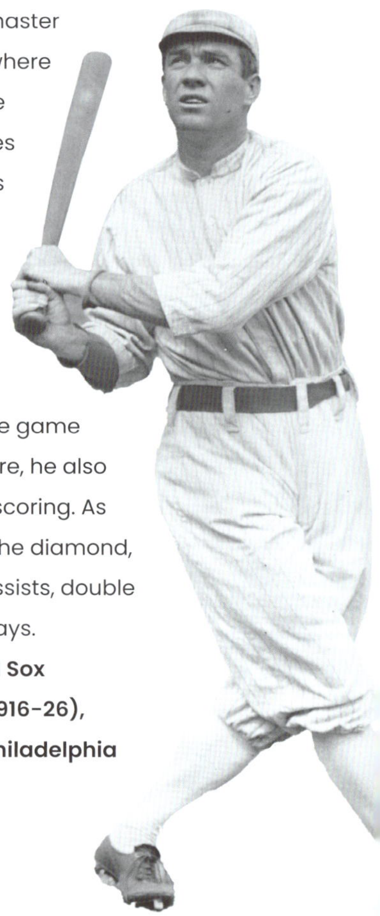

TOM SEAVER

31 Probably the best player in Mets history, Seaver spent the first 11 years of his career with the team and helped them to the 1969 World Series with a Game 4 eight-innings shutout of the Orioles. He picked up the Cy Young Award on three occasions and was a regular All-Star. But his time at Shea Stadium came to an end after he fell out with management, and the Mets offloaded him to Cincinnati. But Seaver wasn't quite done yet. He pitched a no-hitter for his new team and had several more All-Star games before retiring with a 2.86 ERA. When elected to the Hall of Fame in 1992, Seaver received the highest percentage of votes recorded at the time.

Teams: New York Mets (1967-77), Cincinnati Reds (1977-82), New York Mets (1983), Chicago White Sox (1984-86), Boston Red Sox (1986)

ALBERT PUJOLS

30 Pujols played 22 years in the major leagues, picking up two World Series rings, three MVP awards and 11 All-Star appearances. He recorded more than 3,000 hits and 703 home runs with a .296 batting average. But perhaps he'll be best remembered for a stunning debut season in which he was a unanimous choice for Rookie of the Year thanks to his .329 average, 37 home runs and 112 total runs. The secret of Pujols' hitting was his super-consistent swing, a skill that stayed with him right to the end of his career – Pujols had four hits and two home runs in a single game in August 2022, at the ripe old age of 42.

Teams: St Louis Cardinals (2001-11), Los Angeles Angels (2012-21), Los Angeles Dodgers (2021), St Louis Cardinals (2022)

JOHNNY BENCH

29 A single-team player who was team leader of the Big Red Machine – twice World Series Champions in the mid-1970s – Bench was also picked to the All-Star roster on 14 occasions and won the MVP award twice. On defence, he was a star catcher – perhaps the best ever – who rarely let a pitch past and could rocket the ball to base. On offence, he led the National League on runs batted in during three seasons, and was twice the scorer of the most home runs – the first time a catcher had ever managed the feat. Bench's 389 home runs and 1,376 RBI remain the best totals in franchise history.

Team: Cincinnati Reds (1967-83)

DEREK JETER

28 For two decades, Jeter was a lynchpin of the Yankees. He made his debut at the tail end of 1995, when the team was struggling to live up to past glories. The following season, Jeter was installed as starting shortstop and helped the Yankees return to the World Series for the first time in 15 years. They beat the Braves to win the championship, then won three in a row between 1998 and 2000. This era was when Jeter was at his peak – third in the voting for MVP in 1998, career-high numbers in 1999, World Series MVP in 2000. From 2003, Jeter's reliability and consistently was rewarded by being named Yankee team captain, an honour he held until his retirement.

Team: New York Yankees (1995-2014)

CHRISTY MATHEWSON

27 Mathewson pitched at a rate that would make modern players clutch their throwing arms in terror. He was on the mound for at least 266 innings in 14 consecutive seasons, the most memorable of which came in the 1905 World Series. He pitched in Games 1, 3 and 5, and on each occasion the Philadelphia Athletics were unable to score a run. Despite a career 0.97 postseason ERA, the Giants were unable to add to their World Series tally in three consecutive attempts between 1911 and 1913, but Mathewson – their pioneer of pitching – was still good enough to be named one of the first five members of the Hall of Fame in 1936.

Teams: New York Giants (1900-16), Cincinnati Reds (1916)

ALEX RODRIGUEZ

26 The bare statistics put A-Rod up there with the best players ever: .295 batting average, 696 home runs, 3,115 hits, more than 2,000 runs scored and batted in. He was a 14-time All-Star, three-time MVP and a World Series champion. MLB teams recognised his worth and twice awarded him the biggest contract in professional sport history. But A-Rod's career also had a darker side. He was banned for the entire 2014 season after admitting the use of performance-enhancing drugs over a three-year period, and question marks were inevitably cast over the rest of his achievements. A-Rod ended his career as a supremely talented player with a troubled legacy.

Teams: Seattle Mariners (1994-2000), Texas Rangers (2001-03), New York Yankees (2004-13, 2015-16)

ROBERTO CLEMENTE

25 Clemente's impact on MLB was such that the Hall of Fame changed its requirements to allow him to be inducted early. Unfortunately, he became eligible due to his premature death – Clemente died in a plane crash en route to Nicaragua to deliver humanitarian aid. But Clemente isn't just remembered for his tragic end. He was a 15-time All-Star, a two-time World Series champion and MVP in 1966. In the final games of his career, Clemente achieved 3,000 career hits and surpassed Honus Wagner for the most games played in a Pittsburgh Pirates uniform. Clemente was a true legend, both on and off the field.

Team: Pittsburgh Pirates (1955-72)

RANDY JOHNSON

24 Johnson travelled widely in the MLB but wears a Diamondbacks cap in the Hall of Fame – a place he earned in his first season of eligibility thanks to a long career that saw his fastball and tricky slider send many batters back to the dugout frustrated. His high point was probably the 2001 World Series, when the Diamondbacks beat the Yankees despite the New Yorkers being in the unusual position of fan favourite after the 9/11 attacks. Johnson ignored

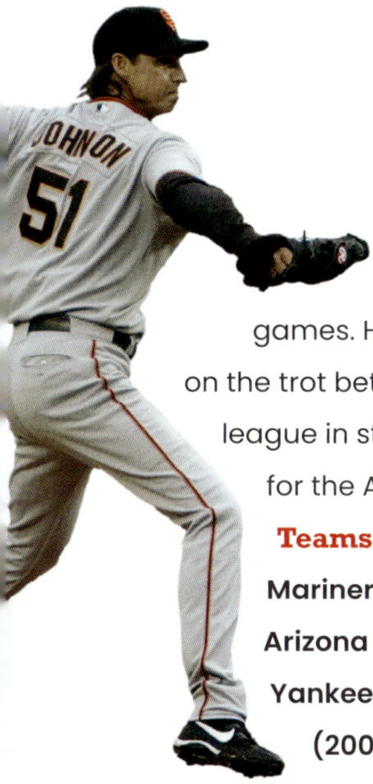

the hype and pitched three winning games. His five Cy Young Awards included four on the trot between 1999 and 2002. He also led the league in strikeouts nine times, and was selected for the All-Star Game on ten occasions.

Teams: Montreal Expos (1988-89), Seattle Mariners (1989-98), Houston Astros (1998), Arizona Diamondbacks (1999-2004), New York Yankees (2005-06), Arizona Diamondbacks (2007-08), San Francisco Giants (2009)

CY YOUNG

23 Young was such a great pitcher that they named the greatest pitcher award after him. He started his career with a mean fastball, and when his pace fell off with age, began throwing with more control. That made him effective into his forties, and he ended his career with many pitching records. Young still has the mark for most career wins with 511, a tally unlikely to be beaten. He also holds the current records for innings pitched, games started and complete games pitched. Young's best period came during his time in Boston, when he won the World Series and pitched a perfect game against the Philadelphia Athletics.

Teams: Cleveland Spiders (1890-1898), St Louis Perfectos/Cardinals (1899-1900), Boston Americans/Red Sox (1901-08), Cleveland Naps (1909-11), Boston Rustlers (1911)

FRANK ROBINSON

22 Robinson has a unique distinction in baseball – the first player to be named MVP for the National League and American League. He earned the NL honour after leading the Reds to the World Series in 1961, then the AL award with the Orioles in 1966 after winning the championship and securing the batting Triple Crown. His 49 home runs that year were a franchise record for 30 years and the most in the American League for a 27-year period. Nicknamed 'The Judge', Robinson delivered harsh verdicts on pitchers across the league. He was also a top outfielder and became the first black MLB manager when he took charge of the Indians in 1975 at the tail end of his career.

Teams: Cincinnati Redlegs/Reds (1956-65), Baltimore Orioles (1966-71), Los Angeles Dodgers (1972), California Angels (1973-74), Cleveland Indians (1974-76)

ROGERS HORNSBY

21 Hornsby's career batting average of .358 is the third-best in MLB history, behind only Ty Cobb and Oscar Charleston. He had three seasons that averaged over .400, including .424 in 1924. He hit 301 home runs and ended his career only 70 hits shy of 3,000. Nevertheless, Hornsby was known as a difficult teammate who didn't bond with his fellow players – perhaps that explains why he moved so often. Still, it took 50 years for a second baseman to score more than Hornsby's 42 home runs in a season, he won the World Series in 1926 with the Cardinals, and he twice secured the batting Triple Crown. Players might not have liked him, but fans sure did.

Teams: St. Louis Cardinals (1915-26), New York Giants (1927), Boston Braves (1928), Chicago Cubs (1929-32), St Louis Cardinals (1933), St Louis Browns (1933-37)

JACKIE ROBINSON

20 After a year in the Negro Leagues following a wartime stint in the Army, Robinson got the call-up that changed both his life and baseball history: Branch Rickey, manager of the Brooklyn Dodgers, signed Robinson for his team. Rickey wasn't just impressed by Robinson's batting and fielding – he thought Robinson also had great strength of character. And he'd need it. Robinson was the first black player to break baseball's colour line, a barrier that had stopped black players since 1884. Robinson's debut was met with a mixed reaction. He had to put up with racial abuse, although many fans embraced both him and supported the end of segregation in MLB. Robinson's selection wasn't just a token gesture. He was a six-time All-Star, won the MVP award in 1949 and helped the Dodgers to World Series glory in 1955. Now, every team has retired number 42 in his honour.

Team: **Brooklyn Dodgers (1947-56)**

MIKE SCHMIDT

19 If you had to pick a single year in which Schmidt was at his best, it would have to be 1980. During this campaign, Schmidt won his only World Series ring and picked up both World Series and MLB MVP awards. But condensing Schmidt's career to a single campaign ignores the longevity of his peak years. During 18 years in Philadelphia, Schmidt was selected to the All-Star Game 12 times. He led the National League eight times in home runs and had the most runs batted in on four occasions. During one remarkable performance against the Chicago Cubs, Schmidt hit four home runs and batted in eight, helping the Phillies come back from an 11-run deficit. Schmidt was also an excellent fielder with a strong throwing arm, and a fast base runner. Put it all together, and it's no surprise most Philly fans consider Schmidt to be their greatest player of all time.

Team: **Philadelphia Phillies (1972-89)**

ROGER CLEMENS

18 No pitcher has won more Cy Young Awards than 'The Rocket'. Clemens generously spread them out among the four teams he represented – three for the Red Sox, two for the Blue Jays, and one each for the Yankees and Astros – but it was with the Yankees alone that Clemens won two World Series rings, in 1999 and 2000. Clemens was unstoppable when his arm felt good. He's still the only player to have twice struck out 20 players in a single nine-inning game, and over the course of his career he gained a 3.12 ERA, 4,672 strikeouts and a .658 winning percentage. Chances are Clemens would be a top ten player of all time were he not accused of taking performance-enhancing drugs in the form of anabolic steroids. Suspicions over his cleanliness prevented Clemens being voted into the Hall of Fame during his ten years of eligibility, despite him successfully disproving the allegations in court.

Teams: **Boston Red Sox (1984-96), Toronto Blue Jays (1997-98), New York Yankees (1999-2003), Houston Astros (2004-06), New York Yankees (2007)**

RICKEY HENDERSON

17 Such was Henderson's love of baseball that he really didn't want to retire, as his long list of teams towards the end of his career proves. But it was in Henderson's four stints with the A's that he was at his best – and the skill he excelled in above all others was base stealing. Henderson ended his career with more than 1,408 stolen bases, nearly 500 more than the next best in MLB history. Henderson's speed and consistency with the bat makes him the GOAT of leadoff hitters, and he earned ten All-Star selections thanks to his prowess at the top of the order. He won two World Series – the first with the A's in 1989, prior to which he was deserved ALCS MVP thanks to him doubling, tripling, hitting two home runs and driving in five runs. Unsurprisingly, the Man of Steal only needed one ballot to sneak into the Hall of Fame.

Teams: **Oakland Athletics (1979-84), New York Yankees (1985-89), Oakland Athletics (1989-93), Toronto Blue Jays (1993), Oakland Athletics (1994-95), San Diego Padres (1996-97), Anaheim Angels (1997), Oakland Athletics (1998), New York Mets (1999-2000), Seattle Mariners (2000), San Diego Padres (2001), Boston Red Sox (2002), Los Angeles Dodgers (2003)**

GREG MADDUX

16 You know you've made it when a stat is named after you. Maddux's pitch control was so perfect that a complete game shutout in fewer than 100 pitches is called a Maddux – he did it 13 times. Maddux was a precise pitcher who never threw the ball more often than required, and it meant his body rarely broke down on him. Maddux won at least 15 games for 17 consecutive seasons between 1989 and 2004, and he became the first pitcher to win four consecutive Cy Young Awards when he picked up the trophy every year from 1992 to 1995. He dominated Game 1 of the 1995 World Series and helped the Braves to the title – a year that he had an unbelievable 19-2 regular season record. He also racked up eight All-Star appearances (missing out in 1993 despite it being a Cy Young season) and was quality in the field too, winning a record 18 Golden Glove awards.

Teams: **Chicago Cubs (1986-92), Atlanta Braves (1993-2003), Chicago Cubs (2004-06), Los Angeles Dodgers (2006), San Diego Padres (2007-08), Los Angeles Dodgers (2008)**

MIKE TROUT

15 At the time of writing, Trout is a three-time MVP and 11-time All-Star – and chances are he'll add more before his career is over. Trout was a unanimous choice for the 2012 Rookie of the Year after breaking numerous records, including the first player in MLB history to hit 30 home runs, steal 45 bases and score 125 runs in a single season. He maintained his run of form for more than a decade, leading the American League in wins above replacement for each of his first five full seasons. As of the start of the 2025 season, he had the best mark for slugging (.581) among all active players and was high on the lists for on-base percentage and stolen base percentage. Such reliability made the Angels offer him a $426 million contract, the second-richest sports history, behind only Lionel Messi. If only Trout had an opportunity for more postseason play – the Angels advanced to the playoffs only once during Trout's first 12 years with the team.

Team: **Los Angeles Angels (2011-present)**

KEN GRIFFEY JR

14 As the son of a major leaguer – Ken Junior even played two seasons with Ken Senior in Seattle – big things were expected of Griffey after he was selected first in the 1987 draft. Luckily, he delivered. Griffey debuted at the age of 19, doubled in his first at-bat, and hit a home run in his first at-bat in Seattle. His almost-perfect left-handed swing collected 630 career home runs (seventh on the all-time list) with 2,781 hits and 1,836 runs batted in. Imagine how many more Griffey might have got had his body not broken down after being traded away from Seattle in 2000. Even so, Griffey can boast of 13 All-Star appearances, ten Golden Gloves, seven Silver Sluggers and the 1997 American League MVP. He was also one of those rare players who was loved by his own team's fans, but also liked by opposing fans. That made him the perfect choice for brands like Nike and Nintendo, who made Griffey the face of baseball in the 1990s.

Teams: Seattle Mariners (1989-99), Cincinnati Reds (2000-08), Chicago White Sox (2008), Seattle Mariners (2009–10)

HONUS WAGNER

13 The Flying Dutchman still has a share in the most National League batting titles, a record he earned in 1911 when he won his eighth and remained unmatched until Tony Gwynn equalled it in 86 years later. Wagner is commonly considered the greatest shortstop of all time, though his teammates said he was an all-rounder who would have excelled no matter what position he was asked to

play. Short and stocky, with a barrel chest and enormous hands, Wagner used his physicality to intimidate pitchers. Statistician Bill James suggests that Wagner had the greatest single season of all time in 1908. Wagner hit .354 with 109 runs batted in at the peak of the dead-ball era, when half as many runs were scored compared to the modern day. He lost the 1903 World Series and many thought Wagner's poor performances cost his team the title, but he redeemed himself in 1909 by outhitting Ty Cobb .333 to .231, helping the Pirates to their first World Series win.

Teams: Louisville Colonels (1897-99), Pittsburgh Pirates (1900-17)

PEDRO MARTÍNEZ

12 According to the Red Sox, Martínez was 5 feet 11 inches and 170 pounds. Few believed it – he seemed like a child on the mound compared with many of his bulky peers. But Martínez made up for a lack of stature with a great fastball and changeup, and he used his weapons to lead the league in strikeouts three times and ERA five times. He won the Cy Young Award three times in four years during one of the highest-scoring eras in history. Martínez's 1.90 ERA during 1999 and 2000 was far superior to the league average of 4.62, and analysis by baseball's stats gurus suggests that Martínez's pitching during those two years was the best since at least 1893. Expos and Red Sox fans

were lucky to see Martínez at his best – and he helped the Red Sox to their World Series win in 2004 – but Martínez was a fine performer at every stop of his career until injuries finally wore him down.

Teams: Los Angeles Dodgers (1992-93), Montreal Expos (1994-97), Boston Red Sox (1998-2004), New York Mets (2005-08), Philadelphia Phillies (2009)

MICKEY MANTLE

11 1956 was Mantle's finest year – he won the Triple Crown with 52 home runs, 130 RBI and a .353 batting average, and was awarded the first of three MVP trophies. But it's difficult to distil Mantle down to one single year. Despite a persistent knee injury suffered in his first MLB season, Mantle dominated baseball in the 1950s and 1960s. He was an All-Star in 16 of the 18 seasons he played, he went to 12 World Series, and he won seven of them. Mantle could blast from both sides of the plate and remains the only player to have 150 home runs batting both left- and right-handed. Mantle reportedly hit some of the longest home runs in MLB history and has come closer than anybody else to hitting the ball out of Yankee Stadium, but he could also refine his game and hit for average. His career batting average is a shade under .300, and he managed just over 1,500 RBI.

Teams: New York Yankees (1951-68)

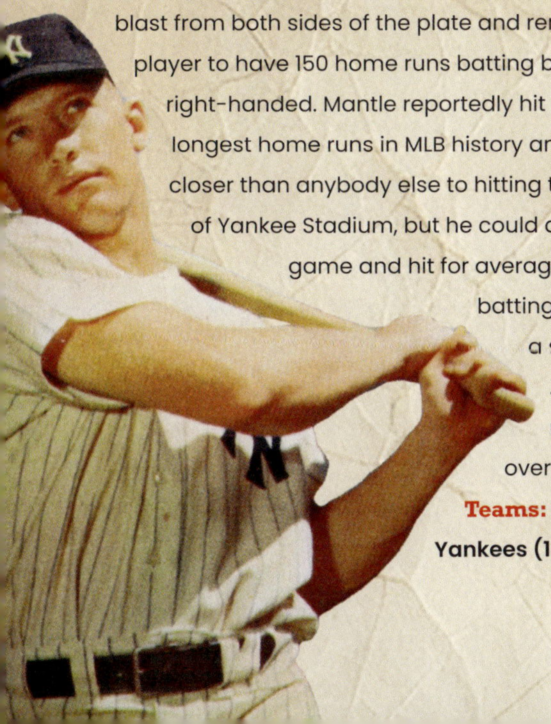

STAN MUSIAL

10 'Stan the Man' was a model of consistency. He could connect bat and ball more than any other player of his era, despite – or perhaps because of – his quirky stance where he turned his back to the pitcher and unwound like a coiled spring. He was an All-Star 24 times, missing out only in his first two years. Were Musial not absent for the 1945 campaign, when he served in the military, he'd likely have had a 25th All-Star selection and would own the outright record – instead, Musial shares it with Hank Aaron and Willie Mays. Musial's batting average was over .300 in each of his first 17 seasons, and he won seven batting titles. He's also second all-time in total bases, third in runs created and fourth in hits. Musial won the World Series three times and had three MVP awards – the last coming in 1948, when he had a .376 batting average, 39 home runs and 131 RBI.

Team: St Louis Cardinals (1941-44, 1946-63)

JOE DIMAGGIO

9 Joltin' Joe spent his entire career with the Yankees and is one of the few names in baseball that people around the world has heard of. Non-baseball fans know him for marrying Marilyn Monroe, but baseball fans know him best for the longest hitting streak in baseball history: 56 games in the summer of 1941. DiMaggio was at his best in the pre-war years, averaging 193 hits and 31 home runs per year. Had the USA not been dragged into the conflagration by Pearl Harbor, he'd have been even higher up the all-time statistical lists. Nevertheless, DiMaggio still played for 13 seasons, made it to ten World Series, and won nine of them – making him the second-most successful player in the sport's history behind his teammate Yogi Berra. So great was DiMaggio's impact on the sport that he was selected as the greatest living player to mark MLB's centenary in 1969 – a title that DiMaggio loved to use for the last 30 years of his life.

Team: New York Yankees (1936-42, 1946-51)

WALTER JOHNSON

8 The greatest pitcher in the history of the game, Johnson amassed statistical records that were unheard of in the dead-ball era. He struck out 3,508 batters – a total that stood for more than 55 years – and still holds the record for most shutouts with 110. The two-time MVP won 417 games with an often-mediocre Senators side, including two 30-win seasons. Between 1910 and 1919, Johnson averaged 26.2 wins a season and had a decade ERA of 1.59. Yet Johnson had to wait until 1924, when he was 38 years old, before he won his only World Series ring – a year in which he also achieved his third and final pitching Triple Crown. Johnson's pitching dominance came from an accurate yet super-quick fastball delivered via a sidearm action – a combination that bamboozled opposing batters who couldn't track the flight of the ball across them. As Ping Bodie put it about facing Johnson, 'You can't hit what you can't see.'

Team: Washington Senators (1907-27)

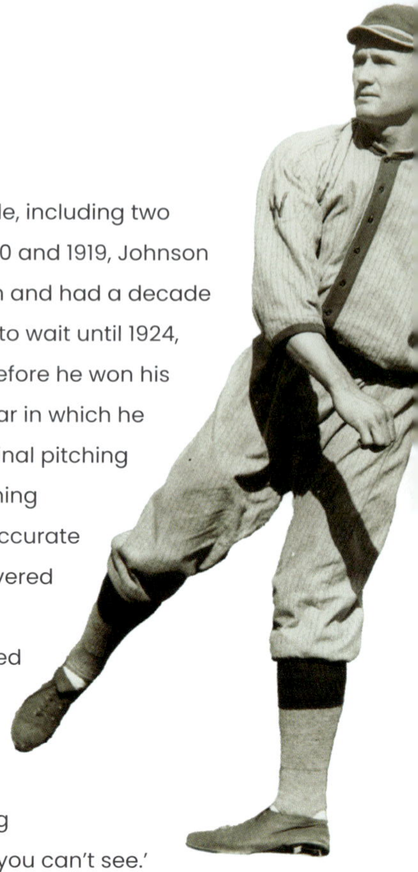

LOU GEHRIG

7 The Iron Horse is best known for two things. First, the way he began a streak of 2,130 consecutive appearances for the Yankees, taking over from a player who benched himself with a headache. Second, the way his streak came to an end, 14 years later: Gehrig could tell that his body was breaking down and voluntarily benched himself, two months before he was diagnosed with ALS. Even today, the fatal condition is better known in the States as Lou Gehrig's Disease. In between, ever-dependable Gehrig

was selected to the All-Star Game seven times, won six World Series rings and was twice the MVP. Gehrig formed a formidable duo with Babe Ruth, hitting 493 home runs, 1,995 RBI and a .340 batting average. He died on 2 June 1941, two years after retiring and making a famous speech at Yankee Stadium in which he declared himself 'the luckiest man on the face of the earth'.

Team: **New York Yankees (1923-39)**

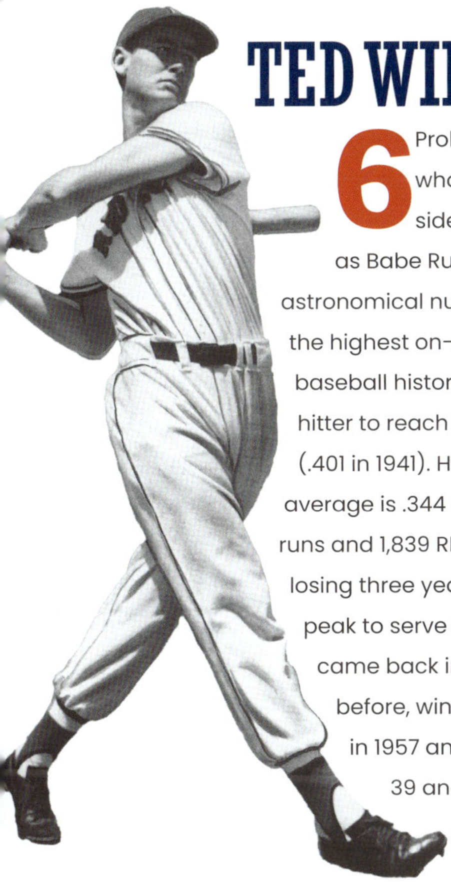

TED WILLIAMS

6 Probably the only player who changed the hitting side of baseball as much as Babe Ruth, Williams put up astronomical numbers. He boasts the highest on-base percentage in baseball history (.482) and was the last hitter to reach a .400 batting average (.401 in 1941). His career batting average is .344 with 2,654 hits, 521 home runs and 1,839 RBI – despite Williams losing three years when he was at his peak to serve in the armed forces. He came back in 1946 just as good as before, winning the AL batting title in 1957 and 1958 and the age of 39 and 40. Williams wrote a book after he retired explaining exactly how he amassed such great statistics. His advice – swinging with a slight uppercut, letting the hips lead and focusing on the parts of the strike zone where hitters can do the most damage – is still preached by coaches today.

Teams: **Boston Red Sox (1939-42, 1946-60)**

BARRY BONDS

5 Few players have a legacy as problematic as Bonds. He was a legendary player, but his performances were made even more spectacular by his use of performance enhancing drugs. Bonds' muscles rippled as he dominated pitchers to win four straight MVP awards between 2001 and 2004 with a style of powerful hitting never seen before, and never has been since. Bonds even broke the single-season home run record in 2001 with 73 homers. The sad thing is, he was a great player before any dubious substances entered his body. Even during his relatively skinny days when there's little chance Bonds was juiced up, he won three MVP awards and was the first name inked onto the All-Star roster. By 2007, the rumours that Bonds was implicated in the BALCO sports doping scandal were growing. During that year, Bonds hit 28 home runs to move to the top of the all-time list, but as his contract expired and he entered free agency, he was arrested by federal investigators. Though he never officially retired, Bonds was effectively blackballed by the league. Hall of Fame electors refused him entry to Cooperstown after he became eligible in 2013, despite Bonds' early-career achievements alone being enough to justify Hall of Fame status.

Teams: **Pittsburgh Pirates (1986-92), San Francisco Giants (1993-2007)**

TY COBB

4 Even in a dead-ball era when batters racked up the hits, Cobb was a hitting machine. He still holds the MLB record for career batting average (.366), is second on the all-time hit list (4,189) and has more batting titles than any other player (12). He recorded better than .400 batting averages in 1911, 1912 and 1922, and in 1911 was named MVP. Cobb spent almost his entire career in Detroit and never won the World Series in three attempts, coming closest in 1909. That 4-3 series defeat to the Pittsburgh Pirates must have hurt, because Cobb also hated to lose. He was renowned for running the bases with more ferocity than any other player in MLB history, spiking players who got in his way for the sheer fun of it. His no-holds-barred style of play meant that his reputation was unfairly trashed by biographers after his death. During his playing career, Cobb was respected, albeit not universally liked. Certainly, he was appreciated enough by the voters who selected the first five players to open the Hall of Fame. Cobb earned 98.2% of votes – only four of 226 electors didn't choose him – giving him a higher percentage than Babe Ruth. As Ruth himself said, 'Cobb is a prick. But he sure can hit. God Almighty, that man can hit.'

Teams: Detroit Tigers (1905-26), Philadelphia Athletics (1927-28)

HANK AARON

3 Despite being known as the man who broke Babe Ruth's career home run record, Aaron didn't top more than 47 in a single season and won only two batting titles. The secret to his unbelievable stats was simple: he hit consistently well over a 22-year career. Aaron is one of only four players with 150 hits in 17 seasons, and he hit 24 home runs in 19 consecutive seasons. He still holds the MLB records for most RBIs (2,297), extra base hits (1,477) and total bases (6,856). Aaron was selected to a record 25 All-Star Games, playing in 24 of them. He hit home run number 715 to surpass Ruth's tally against the LA Dodgers in 1974 and went on to hit another forty during the last years of his career. Aaron held the home run record for 33 years until Barry Bonds surpassed it – although Bonds' drug-enhanced performances mean that many consider Aaron to still be the King of Home Runs. Now, MLB presents the Hank Aaron Award every year to the best offensive player. As the last active MLB player who also played in the Negro League, Aaron also became a civil rights icon and was awarded the Presidential Medal of Freedom by George W Bush in 2002.

Teams: Milwaukee/ Atlanta Braves (1954-74), Milwaukee Brewers (1975-76)

WILLIE MAYS

2 Most great MLB players are power hitters, and there's a few power pitchers who've made it to legendary status too. Mays was neither – he was the most rounded player of them all. Mays sure could hit. He averaged 40 home runs a season between 1954 and 1966, had a .302 batting average and more than 3,000 career hits. But Mays was also a strong base runner, leading the league in stolen bases for four consecutive years from 1956 and scoring more than 2,000 runs. It's fielding that Mays is best known for. He won 12 Golden Glove awards. One play in Game 1 of the 1954 World Series is so famous that it's simply known as 'The Catch'. Mays sprinted towards the centre field fence at the cavernous Polo Grounds, captured Vic Wertz's fly ball over his shoulder, and turned to make a sublime throw that prevented the runners on base from advancing. The Catch has gone down in MLB lore as the moment that tipped the momentum in the World Series, but Mays himself thinks that a bare-handed catch he took against the Pittsburgh Pirates as a rookie was even better. Nevertheless, the 1954 World Series gave Mays his only World Series ring, and he won the first of two MVP awards in the same season.

Teams: **New York/San Francisco Giants (1951-52, 1954-72), New York Mets (1972-73)**

BABE RUTH

1 Red Sox owner Harry Frazee made one of the great misjudgements in sporting history in 1919: he decided his team would be better off without their talented but tempestuous pitcher. Frazee sold Babe Ruth to the Yankees, kicking off an 86-year World Series drought in Boston that became known as the Curse of the Bambino. In New York, Ruth had no regrets about the move. The Yankees knew he was a good pitcher, but Ruth was also unusually handy with the bat – he'd broken the single-season home run record with 29 in his last year at Fenway Park. So, the Yankees decided they'd use Ruth him as a hitter only – and he swatted 54 home runs in 1920. No other player reached 20. Ruth broke his own record another two times, topping out at 60 in 1927, and single-handedly brought he dead-ball era to a close. From now on, baseball was all about offense – scoring more runs rather than strangling opponents from the mound. Ruth ended his career with seven World Series rings and was a 12-time home run leader. His rise from humble origins in a reformatory school to become one of the most famous figures in the Roaring Twenties encapsulates the American Dream and makes Ruth the greatest baseball player in MLB history.

Teams: **Boston Red Sox (1914-19), New York Yankees (1920-34), Boston Braves (1935)**

Getty
MetLife
Armitron
HITACHI
ULTRAVISION
A TOTALLY NEW VISION
adidas
Kodak
399 ft.
408 ft.

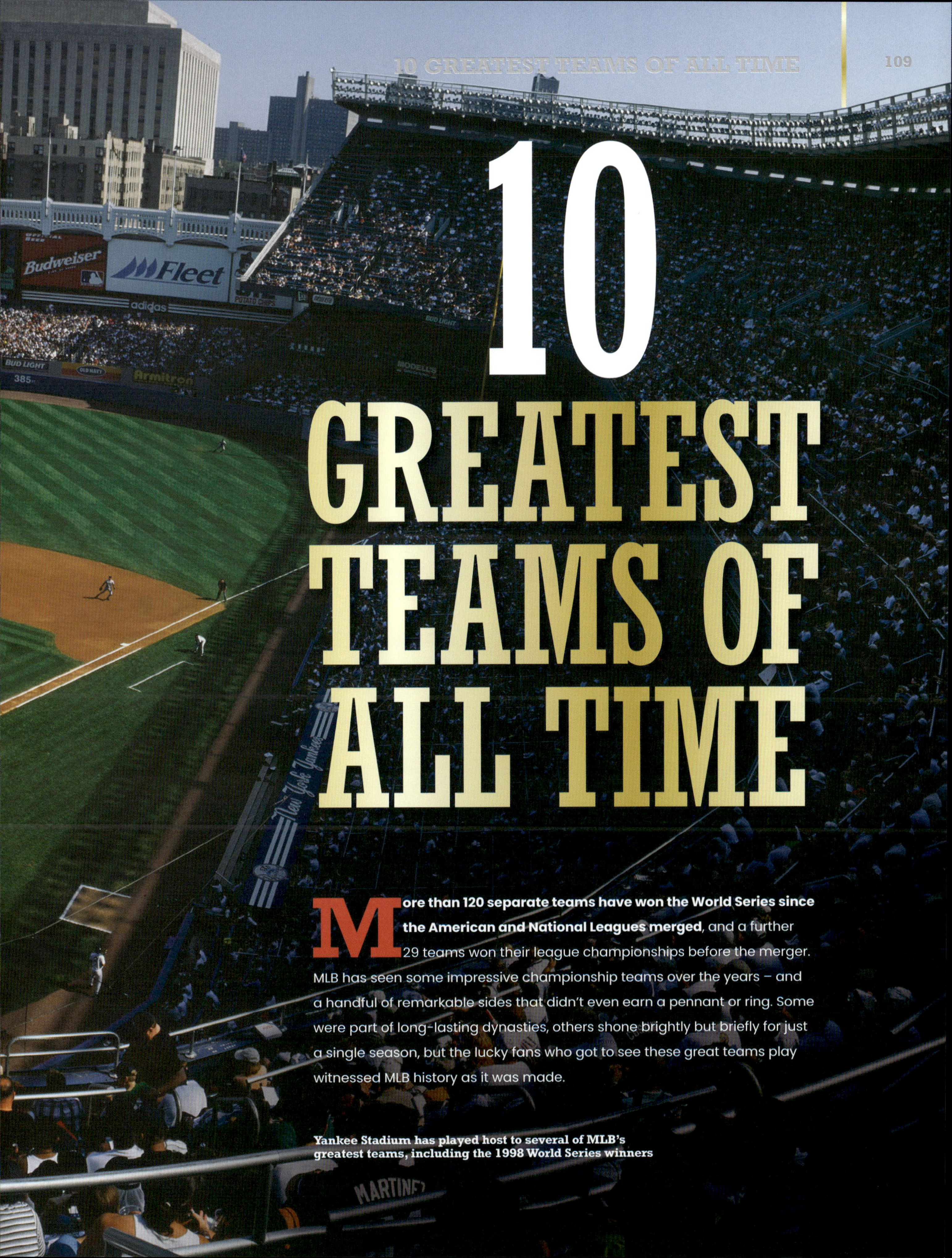

10 GREATEST TEAMS OF ALL TIME

More than 120 separate teams have won the World Series since the American and National Leagues merged, and a further 29 teams won their league championships before the merger. MLB has seen some impressive championship teams over the years – and a handful of remarkable sides that didn't even earn a pennant or ring. Some were part of long-lasting dynasties, others shone brightly but briefly for just a single season, but the lucky fans who got to see these great teams play witnessed MLB history as it was made.

Yankee Stadium has played host to several of MLB's greatest teams, including the 1998 World Series winners

2001 SEATTLE MARINERS

10 The 2001 Mariners didn't win the World Series – they didn't even make it to the World Series. They don't have any Hall of Famers (though Ichiro Suzuki is likely to be voted in when eligible). So how can they qualify as one of the greatest teams of all time? They're one of the best thanks to a record-equalling regular season. They won 116 games to top the AL West by some distance. Of that immense total, 59 came by at least four runs. They didn't just beat teams – they pulverised them.

It was a remarkable turnaround for a team that based its 1990s roster around three stars: Randy Johnson, Ken Griffey Jr and Alex Rodriguez. After those three moved on, the Mariners reloaded with players who lacked allure but bonded well as a team. Second baseman Bret Boone had 37 home runs and 141 runs batted in. Designated hitter Edgar Martínez had 23 home runs and 116 runs batted in. Perhaps most impressive was supposed-rookie Ichiro Suzuki, in his first year playing American baseball, who was named MVP thanks to some stellar performances. Five other Mariners were named to the All-Star Game too.

What happened in the postseason? The Yankees, that's what. The Mariners came up against a New York side motivated by the 9/11 terror attacks. The Mariners lost three close games in the ALCS before it all came crashing down in Game 5 – and it remains the closest the franchise has been to the World Series.

Regular Season Record: 116-46 (.716), **Postseason Record:** 4-6, **Hall of Famers:** 0

Ichiro Suzuki became the second MLB player to win the MVP and Rookie of the Year in the same season

1939 NEW YORK YANKEES

9 In the three seasons from 1936 to 1938, the Yankees won the World Series each year with an average regular season record of 101-52 and a cumulative postseason record of 12-3. They were already one of the best dynasties of all time. Then, in 1939, they got even better.

And it happened while the unthinkable occurred – the Yankees lined up without Lou Gehrig. The man they called the Iron Horse could tell something was not right with his body, and he snapped his record run of 2,130 consecutive starts just eight games into the new season. Despite missing their dependable first baseman, the Yankees went 28-4 in their first 32 games without Gehrig. It propelled the Bronx Bombers to the top of the American League, where they stayed all season. They ultimately finished 106-45 and won the pennant with a 17-game cushion. Joe DiMaggio, Bill Dickey, Joe Gordon and George Selkirk all topped 100 runs batted in and 20 home runs.

Come the postseason, the Yankees faced the Cincinnati Reds in the World Series. It was a quick four-game sweep, lasting only seven hours and five minutes in total. The quality of the Yankee batting was the difference – though both teams had 27 hits, the Yankees walloped seven home runs to the Reds none. By the end of the series, the Yankees had outscored their opponents 20-8 – but it was also the end of an era. After four consecutive World Series appearances, the Yankees dropped to third in the 1940 American League.

Regular Season Record: 106-45 (.702), Postseason Record: 4-0, Hall of Famers: 7 (Bill Dickey, Joe DiMaggio, Lou Gehrig, Lefty Gomez, Joe Gordon, Red Ruffing, Joe McCarthy)

Joe DiMaggio (right) stepped up with .381 batting, 30 home runs and 126 RBI. Joe is seen here with his great rival, Ted Williams

2018 BOSTON RED SOX

8 The Red Sox dominated the 2018 season. They were the first team to 100 wins. They had the batting champion and MVP in Mookie Betts. They had the second-best batter in JD Martínez, who also batted in more runs than anybody else. Chris Sale opened the pitching in the All-Star Game, while Craig Kimbrel acted as his reserve. When the playoffs rolled round, it was no surprise that the Red Sox went into them as the American League's number-one seed.

Even so, the route to World Series success wasn't simple. They faced their old rivals the Yankees in the Divisional Series, and it was a close-run thing at first. The momentum swung in Game 3, when the Red Sox dealt the Yankees their worst-ever margin of defeat in the postseason in a 16-1 demolition. The ALCS matched the Red Sox with the Astros – both 100-win teams – but the Red Sox won four in a row to go to the World Series. There, the Red Sox met another 100-win team in the Dodgers and won in five – their only loss came in Game 3, a battle of attrition in the longest game in World Series history.

There's a slight stain on the Red Sox's best-ever season – the team was later found to have engaged in sign stealing that was 'limited in scope and impact', but nonetheless did enough to cast aspersions as to whether the success the Red Sox enjoyed in 2018 was entirely on the level.

Regular Season Record: 108-54 (.667), **Postseason Record:** 11-3, **Hall of Famers:** 1 (David Ortiz)

Brock Holt became the first person to bat the cycle in a playoff game – hitting a single, double, triple and home run in that order

1902 PITTSBURGH PIRATES

7 At the turn of the 20th century, baseball was undergoing a transition. In 1901, the American League began operation, and some of the National League's best players decided to jump ship. Pirates player-manager Fred Clarke took advantage, persuading his top talent to stay and leading the Pirates to their first pennant. In 1902, they did even better.

Four different players led the league in statistical categories. Centre fielder Ginger Beaumont claimed the batting title with a creditable .357, while pitcher Jack Chesbro led the league with 28 wins. Honus Wagner had the most runs batted in, runs scored, stolen bases and the top slugging percentage. Third baseman Tommy Leach had the most home runs with a scarcely believable six, the lowest total to lead the league in MLB history. The 1902 Pirates conceded only four home runs over the entire season, a sign that baseball was a very different game in the dead-ball era.

On the last day of the season, the Pirates faced the Cincinnati Reds at Exposition Park. The Pirates were light-years ahead in the standings and had already claimed the pennant, but if they won one more game, they'd break the record held by the 1892 and 1898 Boston Beaneaters for the most wins in a season. There were no nerves on display. The Pirates scored three runs in the opening inning and turned the last game into a lap of honour, eventually finishing the game 11-2 to claim their 103rd win and a new major league record.

Regular Season Record: 103-36 (.741), Postseason Record: N/A, Hall of Famers: 3 (Fred Clarke, Jack Chesbro, Honus Wagner)

The 1902 season was the last without a postseason, and the 1903 Pirates would contest the first World Series

The 1906 World Series has gone down as one of the biggest upsets in MLB history

1906 CHICAGO CUBS

6 Under player-manager Frank Chance, who led the team for the first time, the Cubs charged to the top of the National League and stayed there for the season. No team scored more runs, no team conceded fewer. The Cubs ended the pennant race a full 20 games clear of the second-placed New York Giants and with a record 116 wins – a total only matched once in the years since, and that by a team playing eight more times during the regular season. Their .763 regular season winning percentage still stands unbeaten, and possibly will never be beaten.

The team's strength was its pitching. Six members of the rotation had double-digit victories, topped by Mordecai Brown with 26. Brown also set a new MLB record for the lowest earned run average with at least 250 innings pitched – his mark of 1.04 is still the best in the National League. Jack Pfiester and Ed Reulbach also recorded ERAs under 2.00, and Pfiester topped the league in strikeouts. Batting-wise, third baseman Harry Steinfeldt led the National League in both hits (176) and runs batted in (83, tied with the Pirates' Jim Nealon).

It all went wrong in the World Series, when the Cubs lost out to their crosstown rivals, the White Sox. That shock result left the 1906 Cubs with an unenviable label as the best team never to win the World Series. If there was a silver lining to the loss, the Cubs developed chips on their shoulders that sent them into the next two seasons determined to win – and they won the championship both years.

Regular Season Record: 116-36 (.763), Postseason Record: 2-4, Hall of Famers: 4 (Mordecai Brown, Frank Chance, Johnny Evers, Joe Tinker)

1984 DETROIT TIGERS

5 Sparky Anderson's Detroit Tigers were quick out of the blocks in 1984. They'd been a decent team for years, but showed they were the team to beat after winning their first nine games and having a 35-5 record from their first 40, including a record-tying 17-game win streak on the road.

Catcher Lance Parrish led the team in home runs (33) and runs batted in (98), and shortstop Alan Trammell had a decent year with the bat too – his .314 batting average was fifth best in the American League. But the 1984 Tigers were successful thanks to its aces on the mound. Jack Morris won 19 games with a 3.60 earned run average, Dan Petry won 18 games with a 3.24 ERA and seven complete games, and Milt Wilcox did win 17 games with a 4.00 ERA. When the starters began to tire, they were replaced with two great arms from the bullpen. Aurelio López pitched 137 innings, claimed ten games and had a 2.94 ERA. But the standout man was left-handed closer Willie Hernandez. Anderson signed him in preseason, and it was the best deal of his career. Harnandez worked 140 innings with a 1.9 ERA. Thanks to his efforts, Hernandez won both the Cy Young and MVP award.

Hernandez's 32 saves included the series-clinching games in the ALCS, where the Tigers swept the Kansas City Royals, and the World Series, where San Diego Padres were defeated 4-1. In the season finale, outfielder Kirk Gibson hit a three-run home run in the eighth inning and the Tigers ended the year as they began it – with a win.

Regular Season Record: 104-58 (.642), **Postseason Record:** 7-1, **Hall of Famers:** 3 (Jack Morris, Alan Trammell, Sparky Anderson)

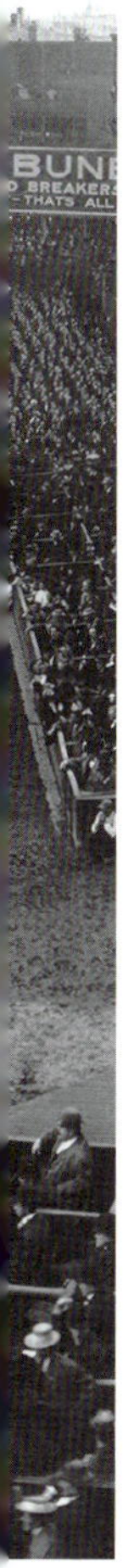

The Tigers scored nine of their 23 runs during the World Series in the first inning

1998 NEW YORK YANKEES

4 Fans who flocked to the 75th year of baseball at Yankee Stadium saw the Bronx Bombers put together one of their greatest seasons. Not that it seemed that way at first. The Yankees lost four of their first five games and manager Joe Torre was reported to be on the hot seat. Torre relied on veteran voices in the dressing room to rally his team – and it worked. The Yankees won 22 of their next 24, steamrollering opposition on their way to 114 victories – then an American League record.

The Yankees quietly amassed wins, going under the radar as countless column inches were dedicated to Mark McGwire and Sammy Sosa's attempt to break the single-season home run record. The Yankees had no need for individual batting heroics. Every player in the lineup could swing a bat, and the Yankees led the majors with 965 runs scored. During the other half of the inning, Yankee pitchers strangled opposition batters. Starter David Cone amassed 20 wins, Orlando Hernandez had a 3.13 earned run average, and David Wells pitched a perfect game. Add in legendary closer Mariano Rivera who had 36 saves and a 1.91 ERA, and the Yankees ended the regular season with a +309 run differential – the best since 1939.

Come the postseason, the Yankees swept the Texas Rangers with a cumulative 8-1 score, defeated Cleveland Indians to win the pennant, then swept the San Diego Padres in the World Series. The Yankees won the next two World Series as well to make it a hat-trick, but neither of the successor teams quite had the same success as the 1998 roster.

Regular Season Record: 114-48 (.704), **Postseason Record:** 11-2, **Hall of Famers:** 4 (Derek Jeter, Tim Raines, Mariano Rivera, Joe Torre)

More than a third of the 1998 Yankees victories were by five runs or more

1970 BALTIMORE ORIOLES

3 The Orioles came into 1970 with a chip on their shoulders. They'd been beaten in the 1969 World Series by the New York Mets in what many pundits regarded as the biggest upsets in postseason history. This time, the Orioles were determined to clinch the championship.

They achieved the first step in that quest easily. They began the season on a five-game win streak, leapt to the top of the AL East, and stayed there all season. The next-nearest Yankees finished 15 games back as the Orioles dominated their regular season opponents from the mound. A trio of pitchers won 20 games or more: Jim Palmer (20 wins, 2.71 ERA), Mike Cuellar (24 wins, 3.48 ERA) and Dave McNally (24 wins, 3.22 ERA). Between them, they helped the Orioles to the best team figures for runs allowed (574) and ERA (3.15).

The only setback was an injury to centre fielder Paul Blair, who was hit by a fastball by Ken Tatum of the California Angels. Blair returned only three weeks after suffering a broken nose, cheekbone and eye socket, and his hitting understandably dropped off. Frank Robinson (25 home runs, 78 RBI), Boog Powell (35 home runs, 114 RBI) and Brooks Robinson (18 home runs, 94 RBI and American League MVP) all stepped up to make up for Blair's struggles.

In the postseason, the Orioles swept the Minnesota Twins in the ALCS, scoring 37 runs in three games. They matched up against the rising Cincinnati Reds in the World Series, winning in five to secure Baltimore's second World Series win.

Regular Season Record: 108-54 (.667), Postseason Record: 7-1, Hall of Famers: 4 (Jim Palmer, Brooks Robinson, Frank Robinson, Earl Weaver)

Despite their reputation as a pitching team, the 1970 Orioles scored 792 runs – the highest in the American League

1976 CINCINNATI REDS

2

The mid-1970s Cincinnati Reds under manager Sparky Anderson were known as the Big Red Machine for the way they steamrollered opposition like an unstoppable runaway train. They dominated the major leagues in 1975 and retained almost every key player to repeat their World Series success in 1976. Just like the year before, the Reds were a championship team carried by their offense, leading the National League in almost every category.

Future all-time hits leader Pete Rose led the team with 215 hits and 130 runs. Hall of Famers Johnny Bench and Tony Pérez contributed 165 runs batted in between them, while their fellow Cooperstown alumnus Joe Morgan had the best season of his career with 27 home runs, 111 RBI and 60 stolen bases. The supporting cast wasn't bad either. Dave Concepción, George Foster, César Gerónimo and Ken Griffey (father of Hall of Famer Ken Jr) all played at least 144 games. Five Reds started the All-Star Game, with another two listed as reserves.

After winning 102 games during the regular season – the best record in MLB and ten games ahead of the Los Angeles Dodgers – the Reds became the only team to go undefeated in the playoffs since the start of divisional play, sweeping both the Phillies and Yankees. The Yankees would go on to win the World Series in 1977 and 1978, so it shouldn't have been a walkover. Even so, the Reds had 42 hits in four games, and only Game 2 was competitive.

Regular Season Record: 102-60 (.630), **Postseason Record:** 7-0, **Hall of Famers:** 4 (Johnny Bench, Joe Morgan, Tony Pérez, Sparky Anderson)

More than 2.6 million fans watched the Big Red Machine play at home in 1976 – a franchise record

1927 NEW YORK YANKEES

1 The 1927 Yankees had one of the most feared batting lineups in baseball history – an attack so potent that terrified pitchers nicknamed it Murderers' Row. Earle Combs and Mark Koenig led off the team, Bob Meusel and Tony Lazzeri batted five and six. Between them came the most famous players of the era: Babe Ruth and Lou Gehrig. Ruth hit 60 home runs and batted in 164 runs. Gehrig had 47 home runs, 218 hits and 175 runs batted in. Given the hard-hitting duo, it's hardly surprising that pitchers just gave up – Ruth and Gehrig combined for 246 walks.

It wasn't just about the offense. The pitching rotation featured Hall of Famers Waite Hoyt (22 wins, 2.63 ERA) and Herb Pennock (19 wins, 3.00 ERA). Urban Shocker (18 wins, 2.84 ERA) also enjoyed one of his best seasons. The whole rotation combined for a team 3.20 ERA and had 11 shutouts.

The Yankees were first in the American League for the entire season and finished 19 games ahead of the Philadelphia Athletics. As soon as it became clear they were on course to win the American League pennant, the attention of the press and nation turned to Babe Ruth's attempt to beat his own single-season home run record of 59. Gehrig actually nudged ahead of Ruth in midseason, but Ruth jumped clear in September, when he hit 17 home runs and broke the record on the last day of the month. The Yankees swept the Pittsburgh Pirates in the World Series, putting a ribbon on the best single-season performance by any team in MLB history.

Regular Season Record: 110-44 (.714), **Postseason Record:** 4-0, **Hall of Famers:** 7 (Earle Combs, Lou Gehrig, Waite Hoyt, Tony Lazzeri, Herb Pennock, Babe Ruth, Miller Huggins)

Despite breaking the home run record, Babe Ruth wasn't eligible for the 1927 MVP award since he'd won it in 1926 and players were barred from winning in consecutive years

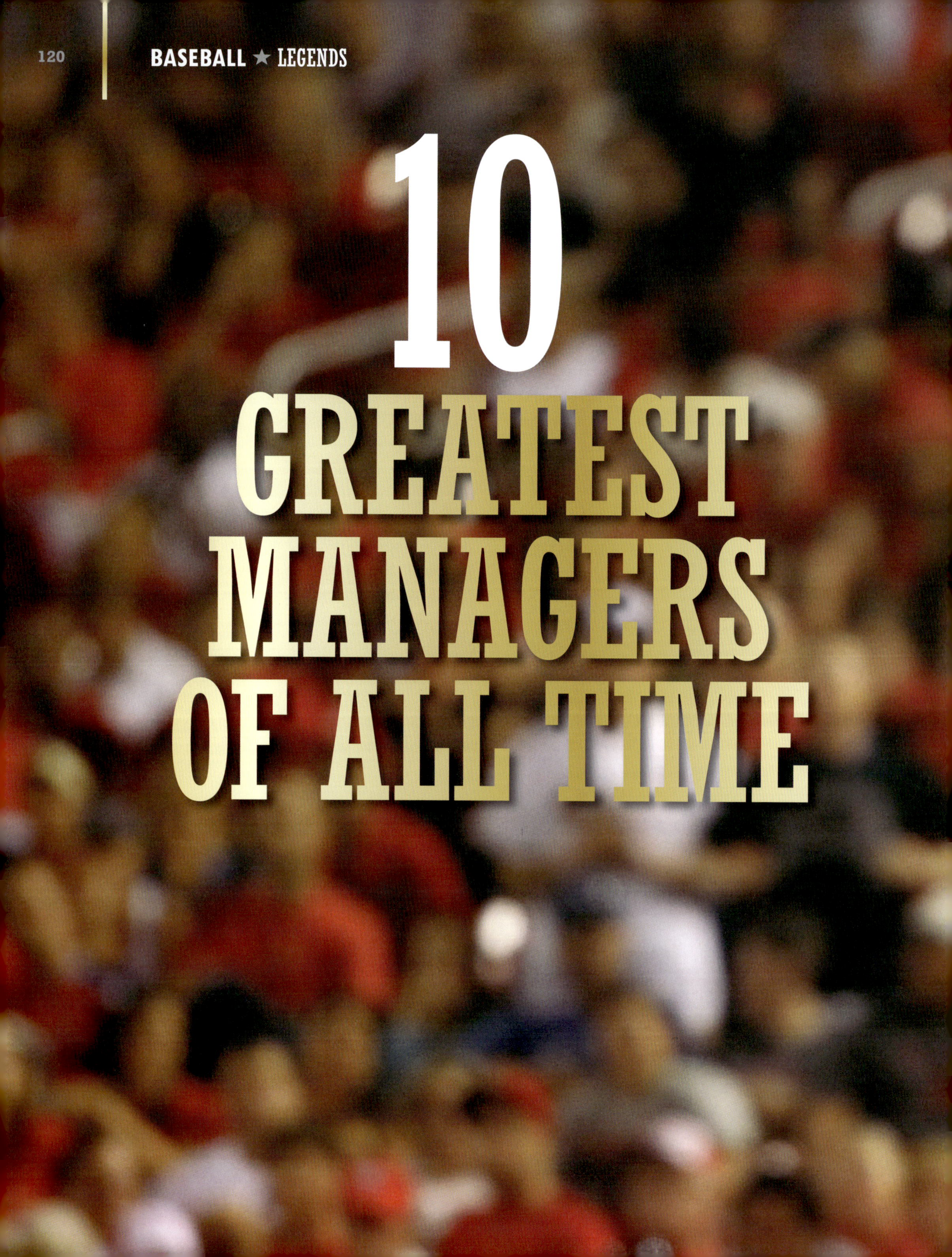

10 GREATEST MANAGERS OF ALL TIME

Baseball success generally comes down to how well pitchers pitch and batters bat. But whether a team wins a pennant or World Series also comes down to how well they are managed. It's a manager's job to train the team, select the lineup, decide on-field strategy and manage a pitcher's workload. Some are also involved in the recruitment and sale of personnel. Essentially, a good manager will help their team rise to the top – and all the managers in this top ten did exactly that. Some were lucky enough to land with the Yankees as they began one of their periods of domination. Others found a long-term home in a different franchise, and several were able to transfer their magic touch between different teams. All are rightfully in the Hall of Fame for their impact on the sport.

Legendary manager Tony La Russa went into retirement on the back of a World Series triumph – only to return to the sport a decade later

JOE TORRE

Not-So-Clueless Joe

10 A manager who had a phenomenal run with the Yankees but didn't enjoy quite as much success elsewhere, Joe Torre helped the Bronx Bombers to four World Series titles in five years, including a three-peat between 1998 and 2000. Prior to his time with the Yankees, Torre had an 894-1,003 managerial record with three teams. Many thought he was better suited to the commentary box – a job he enjoyed for five years after being sacked by the Braves – but the pull of the dugout was too great.

After he was selected to lead the Yankees into the 1996 season, Yankees fans howled in anguish. 'Clueless Joe' wasn't the calibre of manager the Yankees usually looked for. But Torre found his niche at Yankee Stadium. In his first season, he introduced Rookie of the Year Derek Jeter to the team. He reshuffled his pitchers and put Mariano Rivera in as a setup man and closer. Over the next 12 seasons, the Yankees had a winning record every year – their worst was 87-74 in 2000, but they still won the World Series. Torre was named American League Manager of the Year in 1996 and 1998, and only finished out of the top five once. Aside from four World Series wins, they won the American League pennant in 2001 and 2003.

After the Yankees offered him a tight-fisted one-year contract extension, Torre elected to leave New York and take a job in Los Angeles. He led the Dodgers to two division titles in three years before stepping into a job with MLB.

Teams: New York Mets (1977-81), Atlanta Braves (1982-84), St Louis Cardinals (1990-95), New York Yankees (1996-2007), Los Angeles Dodgers (2008-10), Managerial Record: 2326-1997, World Series Wins: 4 (1996, 1998, 1999, 2000)

Torre's 84 postseason wins are the most by any manager in MLB history

CONNIE MACK

The Tall Tactician

9 When Connie Mack began his managerial career, the World Series didn't exist and Babe Ruth hadn't been born. When Mack finished his managerial career, MLB had been formed through the merger of the National and American Leagues, the sport had been transformed through power hitting and Babe Ruth had been dead two years. In the meantime, Mack had managed 7,755 games and earned 3,731 wins – both figures that are still light-years ahead of the next manager in line.

Mack served his apprenticeship as a player-manager with the Pittsburgh Pirates. After four years managing the minor league Milwaukee Brewers, he was headhunted to take charge of the new Philadelphia Athletics in the inaugural season of the American League. He stayed at the helm for fifty years – the longest term as boss of any team in North American professional sport. Mack was an innovator, always willing to try new things and outsmart his opponents on the field of play. Occasionally, this meant he fell out with his players. Shoeless Joe Jackson was traded away from Philadelphia because Mack thought he had a poor attitude and was unwilling to learn. But players who were

The Phillies were criticised as an 'elephant' after losing the 1905 World Series, but Mack defiantly adopted the animal as the Phillies emblem

willing to listen thrived. Future Hall of Famers like Lefty Grove, Eddie Collins and Jimmie Foxx learned their trade under Mack.

Mack created three particularly successful sides. His original team won the American League pennant in 1902 and 1905. A second generation of Mack players won the World Series three times in the 1910s. A third side reached the World Series on three consecutive occasions between 1929 and 1931, winning twice.

Teams: Pittsburgh Pirates (1894-96), Philadelphia Athletics (1901-50), **Managerial Record:** 3731-3948, **World Series Wins:** 5 (1910, 1911, 1913, 1929, 1930)

MILLER HUGGINS

Mighty Mite

8 Cardinals owner Helene Hathaway Britton wasn't keen on manager Roger Bresnahan's brash personality, so she let him go after the 1912 season and gave the job to 34-year-old second baseman Miller Huggins instead. Huggins helped the Cardinals finish above .500 in two of his five seasons, enough for him to get appointed by the Yankees.

It was in New York that Huggins benefited from an enormous stroke of luck. Team owner Jacob Ruppert met with the owner of the Boston Red Sox and agreed a deal for their power-hitting pitcher-infielder, Babe Ruth. With the Babe in pinstripes – and having fully transitioned from a pitcher to a hitter – the Yankees won at least 94 games in each of the next four seasons. They secured the American League pennant in 1921 and 1922 and won the World Series title in 1923.

Perhaps Huggins' greatest skill was his ability to infuse new blood into a successful side without disturbing the balance. It meant the Yankees kept winning year after year. Once Lou Gehrig and Earle Combs joined the team, the Yankees were practically unstoppable. They enjoyed a 302-160 record between 1926 and 1928. The 1928 World Series winners subsequently had nine players elected to the Hall of Fame – and Huggins joined them at Cooperstown. The Yankees boss would probably have won more than his three World Series rings were it not for his early death at the age of 51, in the middle of the baseball season.

Teams: St Louis Cardinals (1913-17), New York Yankees (1918-29), **Managerial Record:** 1413-1134, **World Series Wins:** 3 (1923, 1927, 1928)

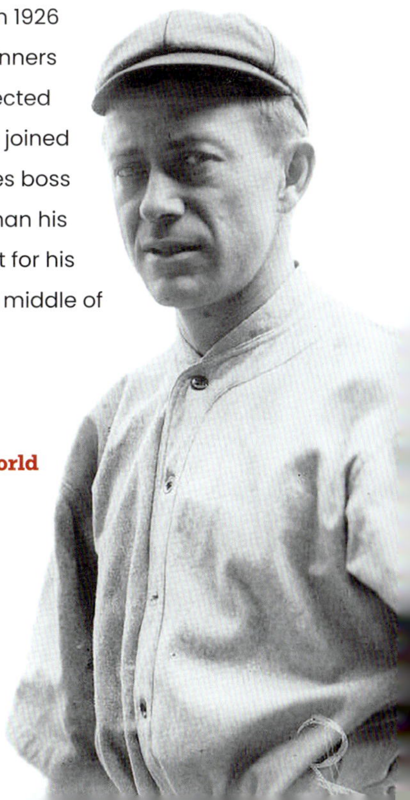

Though the two often clashed, Babe Ruth claimed that Huggins was the only person who knew how to keep him in line

BOBBY COX

Mr Atlanta

7 Bobby Cox's first stint with the Braves saw him rebuild a failing team, giving them their first winning season for years. Braves owner Ted Turner fired him in 1981 and immediately regretted the decision. When asked who was on his shortlist to replace Cox, Turner replied, 'It would be Bobby Cox if I hadn't just fired him. We need someone like him around here.' Cox moved on to the Blue Jays instead and took the team to their first ever division title.

But Cox had unfinished business in Atlanta and rejoined the Braves as general manager in 1985. After the team sank back to the bottom of their division, Cox decided to take the reins for a second time. He inherited a talented roster that he'd personally built in the draft and took the Braves from last to first in the National League. The fairytale season didn't quite come to fruition – another last-to-first team, the Minnesota Twins, won the World Series – but Cox had sown the seeds of a dynasty. Apart from the strike-shortened 1994 season, Atlanta won the NL East every year between 1991 and 2005. Six times they breached the 100-win barrier. Add in Cox's playoff appearances in 1985 and 2010, and he's has been to the playoffs more times than any other MLB manager. If there's flaws in Cox's career, it's that he only won the World Series once in 16 postseason campaigns – and that he holds the MLB record for the most ejections with 161.

Cox is a four-time MLB Manager of the Year, one of only four bosses to have won it in both American and National Leagues

Teams: **Atlanta Braves (1978-81), Toronto Blue Jays (1982-85), Atlanta Braves (1990-2010), Managerial Record: 2504-2001, World Series Wins: 2 (1977, 1995)**

CASEY STENGEL

The Ol' Perfessor

6 Casey Stengel was announced as the next Yankee manager on 12 October 1949, 25 years to the day that he hit a home run against the Yankees in the World Series. But he was an odd choice for boss of a franchise that demanded success. During his playing career, Stengel had a reputation for clowning around and butting heads with management. When he tried out as a manager in his own right with the Dodgers and Braves, Stengel's teams were mediocre. Still, Yankee general manager George Weiss must have identified something in Stengel – and results would soon prove him right.

Few people expected immediate success. The Yankees were in transition and Joe DiMaggio, the team's star player, was expected to miss most of the season due to injury. But Stengel shuffled the young charges on his roster and began building a dynasty. The Yankees won five consecutive World Series as Stengel introduced new blood in the form of pitcher Whitey Ford and power hitter Mickey Mantle.

Stengel's Yankees won another two World Series over the next seven years, and were defeated in the season finale on three other occasions. After leaving the Yankees, Stengel was hired as the first manager

Stengel compiled a 1905-1842 record as manager – but his tally with the Yankees was a much more impressive 1845-1149

of a new New York team when the Mets joined the major leagues as an expansion franchise. It was a very different experience. Stengel's team were often on the end of punishing scorelines, but their famous manager's charisma won over fans to the Mets cause.

Teams: Brooklyn Dodgers (1934-36), Boston Braves (1938-43), New York Yankees (1949-60), New York Mets (1962-65), **Managerial Record:** 1905-1842, **World Series Wins:** 7 (1949, 1950, 1951, 1952, 1953, 1956, 1958)

SPARKY ANDERSON

Captain Hook

5 The Cincinnati Reds were already a decent team when relatively unknown minor-league boss Sparky Anderson got the job, but they kicked into an even higher gear with him at the realm. The Big Red Machine won 1,475 games under his watch with a winning percentage not far short of .600. They qualified for the playoffs five times in nine seasons, winning the World Series in 1975. The following year, the Reds retained the title in a famous postseason that saw them dominate in October, winning seven playoff games out of seven. Anderson had a reputation for being a demanding leader. He pulled starting pitchers at the first sign of weakness – giving rise to the nickname Captain Hook – and required power hitters Pete Rose, Johnny Bench and Joe Morgan to maintain their terrific batting stats for season after season.

After his time in Cincinnati came to an end, Anderson moved on to Detroit, where he stayed for the next 17 years. Although he wasn't as consistently successful there, his Detroit teams still amassed a .516 winning percentage and a winning record in each of his first 11 years. The Tigers progressed to the playoffs twice, and their biggest success under Anderson came in the 1984 postseason. Memories of the Reds' 1976 campaign returned when Anderson's Tigers won the World Series with a 7-1 record during the playoffs. With that win, Anderson became the first manager to win the World Series in both the American and National Leagues.

Teams: Cincinnati Reds (1970-78), Detroit Tigers (1979-95), **Managerial Record:** 2194-1834, **World Series Wins:** 3 (1975, 1976, 1984)

Anderson was manager in all three seasons that the Reds won more than 100 regular season games

TONY LA RUSSA

A Trio of Tonies

4 Whereas some managers only achieved great things at one club, Tony La Russa was a winner in all three cities he managed. He won 51.2 percent of games in Chicago, 54.3 percent in Oakland and 54.4 percent in St Louis. He took all three teams to the postseason and won the World Series with the Athletics and the Cardinals, joining Sparky Anderson as the only managers to have won the World Series with both American and National League teams.

La Russa's best spell came as the boss of the Bash Brothers in Oakland between 1988 and 1990. He managed a potent attack comprising Jose Canseco, Mark McGwire and Rickey Henderson, guiding them to 306 wins in three seasons and three consecutive American League pennants. The Athletics won the World Series in the middle of those years, recording a whitewash against the San Francisco Giants and a cumulative 32-14 scoreline.

In St Louis, La Russa had an equally powerful attack with Albert Pujols bashing the ball out of the park. La Russa took the Cardinals to the postseason nine times in 16 years, winning the World Series in 2006 and 2011. After getting his second Cardinal World Series ring, La Russa chose to retire at his peak – but he returned after a decade, when the White Sox came calling again. At 76 years old, many thought La Russa was past it, but he took the White Sox to the top of the AL Central before retiring a second time.

Teams: Chicago White Sox (1979-86), Oakland Athletics (1986-95), St Louis Cardinals (1996-2011), Chicago White Sox (2021-22), **Managerial Record:** 2902-2515, **World Series Wins:** 3 (1989, 2006, 2011)

La Russa put together an impressive career playoff record of 71-61

WALTER ALSTON

Smokey

3 Walter Alston is in the unusual position of winning World Series with teams in different cities – yet for the same franchise. Before Alston, the Dodgers had never won the MLB championship title. They had come close many times, representing the National League seven times, but lost on every occasion. That changed in 1955 – Alston's second season at the helm – when the Dodgers clinched the pennant earlier than any team had before, with a 92-46 record. In the World Series, Alston started struggling pitcher Johnny Podres twice, and he won both times. Breakout star Sandy Koufax wasn't asked to pitch at all, but the future Hall of Famer would do plenty in the years that followed.

In 1958, the Dodgers relocated from Brooklyn to Los Angeles. Alston made the cross-country move with his team, and history repeated itself. In his second season in the new city, the Dodgers had a World Series-winning campaign. This time Koufax was asked to pitch, though he lost his only start. It was youngster Don Drysdale who led the team from the mound with 17 wins over the season, including one in the World Series. The Dodgers also won the World Series in 1963 and 1965.

By the time Alston retired in 1976, he had won more than 2,000 games. He also left behind a Dodgers organisation in great shape. After Alston departed, his successor Tommy Lasorda led the Dodgers to the World Series in three of his first five seasons.

Teams: Brooklyn/Los Angeles Dodgers (1954-76), Managerial Record: 2040-1613, World Series Wins: 4 (1955, 1959, 1963, 1965)

Alston led the Dodgers for 23 years, but never had more than a one-year rolling contract

JOHN McGRAW

Little Napoleon

2 John McGraw had a tough start to his managerial career. He was named player-manager of the Orioles in 1899 and kept them in the race for the National League pennant, but the illness and death of his wife took him away from the team and they dropped to fourth place. Then, the Orioles folded and disappeared from the major leagues. When they reformed ahead of the 1901 season, McGraw was rehired as player-manager.

McGraw's best work came when he returned to the National League with the New York Giants, who he managed for almost 30 years. During that time, he had three particularly golden periods. Early on, between 1904 and 1906, he went 307-151-8. The Giants won the 1904 pennant and the 1905 World Series. After a brief lull, McGraw's Giants won 303 games and three consecutive pennants between 1911 and 1913, though they failed to win the World Series. Between 1921 and 1924, the Giants won four pennants in a row, going on to win the World Series in 1921 and 1922. They came close in 1924 too, losing Game 7 of the World Series in extra innings.

Between those golden periods, the Giants were still a good team. Only four times did McGraw's Giants fail to record a winning season with him at the helm, and two of those were his first and final seasons when he wasn't there for the whole campaign. Add it all up, and McGraw holds the best win-loss differential in MLB history with 815.

Teams: Baltimore Orioles (1899, 1901-02), New York Giants (1902-32), Managerial Record: 2763-1948, World Series Wins: 3 (1905, 1921, 1922)

Only Casey Stengel can match McGraw's ten pennants won as a manager

JOE McCARTHY

Master Joe

1 Perhaps the greatest argument in support of Joe McCarthy being the best manager in MLB history is that he never had a losing record. In 24 seasons across three teams, he was always a contender. Granted, he had some serious talent to work with. His first side was a Cubs outfit with Rogers Hornsby and several future Hall of Famers, and they won the National League pennant in 1929. With the Yankees, McCarthy inherited a roster that included Babe Ruth and Lou Gehrig. Over the next 15 years, his Bronx Bombers dominated baseball. Although the Red Sox were the one team McCarthy didn't take to the World Series, he came close in 1948 and 1949 with Ted Williams leading the side.

It's with the Yankees that McCarthy will always be associated. McCarthy won seven World Series titles, making it seem easy – so easy, in fact, that some detractors claim that anybody could have managed the Yankees to success when they had such a talented pool of players. But McCarthy's strength was his man-management. Although quiet and unassuming, McCarthy mostly kept a temperamental Babe Ruth in line, and charismatic superstar Joe DiMaggio continued to focus on baseball even when fame came calling.

McCarthy shares some of his MLB records. He's tied for World Series wins with Casey Stengel. His six 100-win seasons are matched by Bobby Cox. But he has the best regular-season winning percentage (.615) and the best postseason winning percentage (.698). And when all the evidence is put on the table, McCarthy is nearly always the consensus choice for the best manager in MLB history.

Teams: Chicago Cubs (1926-30), New York Yankees (1931-46), Boston Red Sox (1948-50), **Managerial Record:** 2125-1333, **World Series Wins:** 7 (1932, 1936, 1937, 1938, 1939, 1941, 1943)

McCarthy's teams never finished lower than fourth place in the American or National League

10 GREATEST SERIES OF ALL TIME

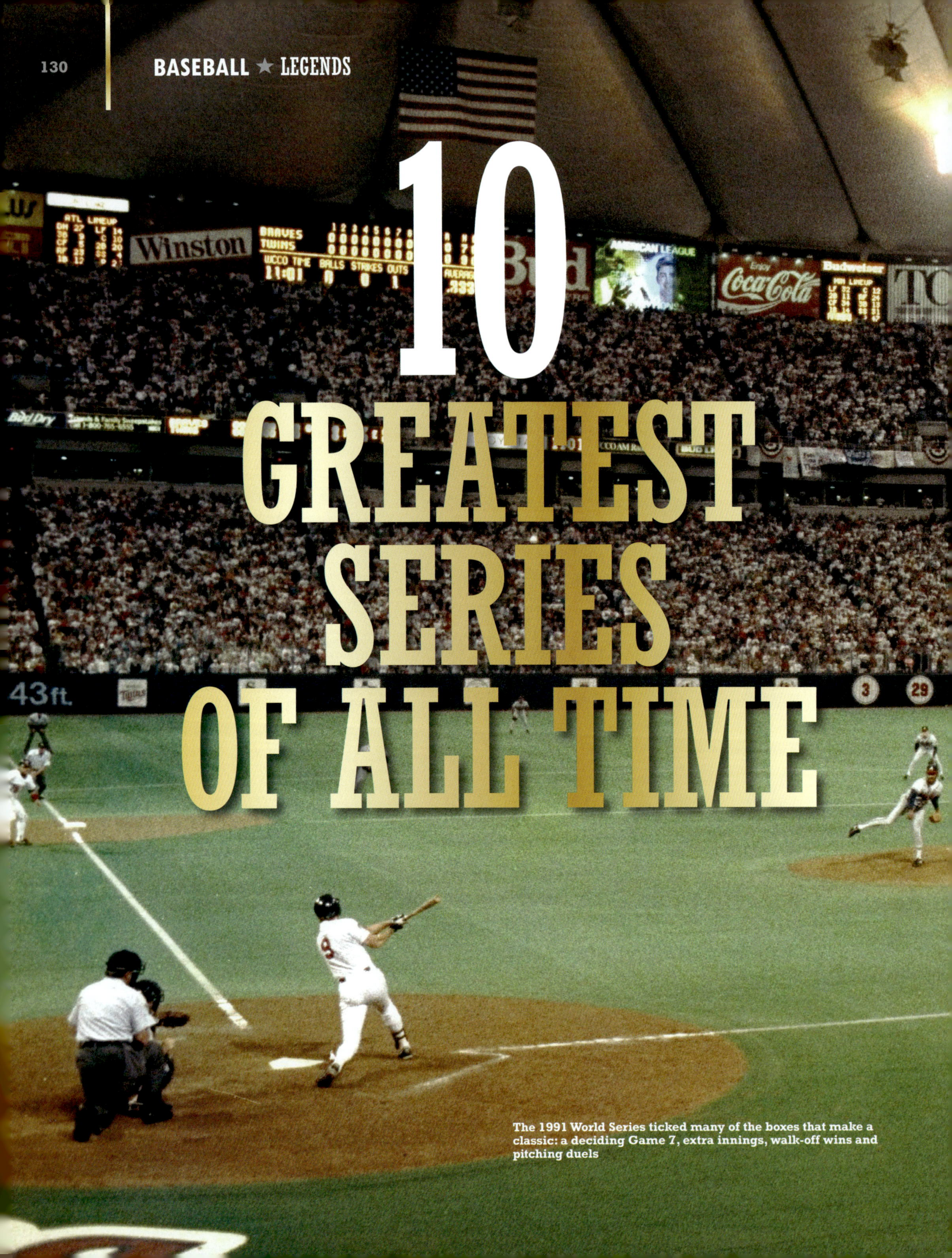

The 1991 World Series ticked many of the boxes that make a classic: a deciding Game 7, extra innings, walk-off wins and pitching duels

When the MLB postseason begins, every playoff series becomes an eliminator. Every team that makes it this far has played more than 100 games, but if they can't do the business in these crucial fixtures, it'll all be for nothing. Such high stakes means that players put it all on the line, and that often results in some classic matchups. Here's our pick of the greatest postseason clashes – iconic faces making unforgettable plays in the quest to win the World Series.

The Cubs win meant that their opponents gained the unwanted record of longest World Series drought, having last won in 1948

108-YEAR WAIT

10 The last time the Cubs won the World Series, it was the fifth edition of the season finale. Now, they were in World Series number 112 – but they finally ended the longest championship drought in American pro sports with a tense, seven-game battle. The two teams split Games 1 and 2 in Cleveland before a mammoth pitching duel took place under the lights of Wrigley Field in Game 3. In the end, only a solitary run was scored – it came for the Indians off a ball thrown by Carl Edwards Jr.

It all came down to a decisive Game 7 at Progressive Field. The Cubs led from the opening inning to the eighth, but Rajai Davis hit a game-tying home run off Aroldis Chapman and the game ended all-square at 6-6. The tension ramped up during a 17-minute rain delay, but Cubs right fielder Jason Heyward used the pause in proceedings to rally his team, telling them 'We're the best team in baseball for a reason. Stick together and we're going to win this game!'

His teammates listened. During the first at-bat after play resumed in the tenth inning, Kyle Schwarber led off with a single. Ben Zobrist and Miguel Montero both drove in runs to give Chicago an 8-6 lead. The Indians responded with a one-run single, before Kris Bryant nervously fielded a ground ball to bring the game – and the Cubs' long World Series wait – to an end.

Series: 2016 World Series, **Teams and Scores:** Chicago Cubs 4, Cleveland Indians 3

BACK TO BLACK

9 The 1952 World Series brought together two of MLB's biggest teams and many of the sport's most famous stars. The Yankees had Yogi Berra and Mickey Mantle. The Dodgers had Jackie Robinson. But the spotlight was unexpectedly cast on Joe Black in Game 1. Black had spent eight years pitching in the Negro Leagues before the Dodgers signed him prior to the 1952 season, and he emerged as a league-leading relief pitcher. Still, nobody expected Black to be named starter in Game 1 – but he threw all nine innings, striking out six Yankees as the Dodgers triumphed 4-2. Black was also asked to take on starting duties in Game 4 and lasted until the eighth inning, but the Yankees won that one 2-0.

By the time the two teams tied the series at 3-3 to take it to a deciding Game 7, the Dodgers had firmly nailed their colours to the mast and Black was given the ball for his third game as starter. Unsurprisingly, he was fatigued. Black only lasted five innings and left the game having conceded three runs. The Dodgers were still in the game and might have taken the lead in the seventh inning when Jackie Robinson connected bat on ball with the bases loaded. Instead, second baseman Billy Martin sprinted in from deep and caught the ball off his shoelaces. The Yankees wrapped up the game 4-2 to win their fourth World Series in a row – tying their own record from the 1930s.

Series: 1952 World Series, Teams and Scores: New York Yankees 4, Brooklyn Dodgers 3

The Yankees' Mickey Mantle scored his first World Series home runs in 1952 – he ended his career with a record 18

THE GREATEST GAME

David Freese was named World Series MVP after his game-winning walk-off

8 Baseball fans remember the 2011 World Series for its back-and-forth Game 6. The Rangers had one hand on the trophy at the bottom of the ninth when David Freese came on to bat and got down a 1-2 count. If pitcher Neftalí Feliz threw another strike, the game and series would be over with the score 7-6. But third baseman Freese didn't stick to the script. He hit a two-run triple over the head of a jumping Nelson Cruz to tie the game.

After Freese's heroics, the momentum see-sawed between the two teams during extra innings. The Rangers went ahead again in the tenth inning, only for the Cardinals to claw back the deficit. A sign of the Cardinals' desperation was shown when a pitcher was used as a pinch hitter for another pitcher – and was then replaced by a different pinch-hitting pitcher. Then Freese stepped into the box once again in the 11th inning and sent Busch Stadium into a frenzy with a walk-off home run, banging the ball directly through centre field. Never again would Freese have to buy a drink in St Louis – a fact confirmed the next day when he batted in two runs to hand the Cardinals the World Series trophy.

However, the 2011 World Series was more than just one game. Games 1 and 2 were both decided by one run, while Albert Pujols hit three home runs in Game 3 – a deed only ever accomplished twice before, by Babe Ruth and Reggie Jackson.

Series: 2011 World Series, Teams and Scores: St Louis Cardinals 4, Texas Rangers 3

GRAND SLAM SINGLE

7 Not every classic series needs to go to seven games. The 1999 NLCS was close throughout its six games. Atlanta won Game 1 by a score of 4-2 – and by the end of the series, that two-run margin would seem cushy. The next five were all decided by one run. Atlanta won the next 4-3, then took Game 3 with a tight 1-0. The Mets kept the series going with 3-2 and 4-3 victories in Games 4 and 5 – and the second of those wins came in the 15th inning. The Mets were staring down a loss after conceding a run at the top of the inning, but with the bases loaded, Robin Ventura hit a home run to seal victory. It should have been a grand slam, but Ventura was mobbed by his teammates and never rounded the bases, so the score was recorded as a quirky 'gland slam single'.

Only then was the stage set for a rollercoaster Game 6. It ended 8-8 with two exhausted bullpens, but the pitchers were required to come back out and perform in extra innings. Both teams burned through their relievers and pinch hitters and scored a run in the tenth innings, but the Braves and Mets still couldn't be separated. Finally, in the 11th, the tired Mets pitchers lost control. Kenny Rogers was given the ball, but the Braves loaded the bases, and Rogers gave away a walk-in run that awarded Atlanta the National League pennant and a spot in the World Series.

Series: **1999 National League Championship Series,**
Teams and Scores: **Atlanta Braves 4, New York Mets 2**

The 1999 NLCS saw a team come from behind to take the lead in the eighth inning on three different occasions

FROM THE ASHES

6 The Yankees went into the 2001 season looking for their fourth straight championship win, and everything seemed to be going their way – until the MLB season ground to a halt after 9/11 attacks stunned New York and the nation. After the disaster, the Yankees stumbled into the playoffs, but found their form again to defeat the 116-win Mariners in the ALCS and progress to the World Series against the Diamondbacks.

The Diamondbacks took a 2-0 lead in the first two games, but the series came to life during the first game at Yankee Stadium. In an emotional night, President George W Bush threw out the ceremonial first pitch. Roger Clemens then took to the mound and held firm to secure a 2-1 win for the Yankees. In the next game, Derek Jeter continued to develop his reputation as Mr November with a walk-off home run in the tenth inning to tie the series. Alfonso Soriano then gave the Yankees a 3-2 series lead with a walk-off single in the 12th inning of Game 5.

The Diamondbacks won the next to send the World Series to Game 7 – and it was a remarkable end to a remarkable series. Down 2-1 in the bottom of the ninth, Arizona had to face the greatest Yankee closer of all time in Mariano Rivera. But Rivera recorded a rare loss after Tony Womack doubled to tie the game, then Luis Gonzalez hit a scoring single to centre field. It was enough to win the game and prevent New York's post-9/11 fairytale ending.

Series: 2001 World Series, Teams and Scores: Arizona Diamondbacks 4, New York Yankees 3

President Bush's ceremonial first pitch was thrown while wearing a bulletproof vest and with an armed secret service agent disguised as an umpire

The 1986 Red Sox were one good pitch away from victory

THE ONE-PERCENTERS

5 At one point in the 1986 World Series, the Mets were given a 0.8% chance of winning the title. Despite the Mets having a much better winning percentage in the regular season, it was the Red Sox who took the first two games. The Mets won Games 3 and 4, but the Red Sox put the New Yorkers under pressure in Game 5 and earned a 4-2 win.

It was in the next fixture that the Mets' chances of winning dropped to less than 1 in 100. The Mets found themselves batting in the bottom of the tenth inning, trailing by two runs, down 3-2 in the series, with two players out. The comeback began when Gary Carter singled to get on base, then Kevin Mitchell singled to join him. Next, Ray Knight singled to load the bases. The game was tied up when Bob Stanley batted in two of the runners, then Red Sox first baseman Bill Buckner fluffed a simple ground ball and allowed Knight in for the game-winning run. The unlikely victory tied the series and sent both teams into a winner-takes-all Game 7.

Momentum had swung, and now the Mets were in the driving seat. In the decider – the 500th World Series matchup – the Red Sox held their opponents scoreless for the first five innings, but the Mets finally found their groove and demolished the Red Sox bullpen with eight runs in their final three.

Series: **1986 World Series,** **Teams and Scores:** **New York Mets 4, Boston Red Sox 3**

WALTER'S WORLD

4 The 1924 World Series started strongly, with a 12-inning marathon in which legendary pitcher Walter Johnson – making his first World Series appearance as a 36-year-old veteran – finished on the losing team while pitching the complete game. But the series was far from over, and the Senators drew level in the next game. It would become a familiar pattern. The Giants went 2-1 up after Game 3 before the Senators levelled in the next, then the Giants went 3-2 up – again beating Johnson, who again pitched a complete game – before the Senators levelled up one more time and the series went to Game 7.

The Senators had tried starting their best pitcher, but it had failed twice. This time, player-manager Bucky Harris opted for something different. He unexpectedly started right-hander Curly Ogden – but it was only a decoy, and Ogden was pulled after only two batters in favour of lefty George Mogridge. The subterfuge worked, at least at first. The Giants didn't score until the sixth inning, although they scored three runs in short succession and the Senators saw their chances slipping away. They managed to tie the game in the eighth, then called upon Walter Johnson as an emergency reliever. Johnson ended up pitching four innings as the game went into extra innings and, despite his earlier travails in the series, didn't concede a single run. When the Giants made costly fielding errors as their players began to tire, Muddy Ruel ran in the World Series-winning run.

Series: **1924 World Series,** Teams and Scores: **Washington Senators 4, New York Giants 3**

As well as pitching a complete Game 1, Giants pitcher Art Nehf also ran in a score for his team

BATTLE OF THE UNDERDOGS

3 After the first two games, nobody had this down as one of the greatest World Series of all time. The Twins won both in front of sellout crowds at home, and Minnesotans hoped that their team might wrap up the series in Atlanta. It wasn't to be. The Braves got their first win with a walk-off victory in Game 3 after Mark Lemke batted in the crucial run. Next, the Braves captured two more wins at home to take a 3-2 series lead.

Minnesotans did have a chance to see World Series baseball again, after all – and both games went to extra innings. Kirby Puckett played the hero in Game 6 with a game-winning home run in the 11th inning to send the series to Game 7. And what a Game 7. In one of the best pitching duels of all time, Braves starter John Smoltz lasted into the seventh innings while the Twins' Jack Morris looked like he'd never give up. By the end of regulation time, both teams were still scoreless.

At the start of the tenth inning, Twins manager Tom Kelly wanted to pull Morris from the mound – but Morris felt he could keep going. Pitching coach Dick Such backed his player. Kelly grudgingly gave in with a famous understatement: 'Oh hell. It's just a game.' The gutsy call paid off, as Morris continued his shutout for one more inning and pinch hitter Gene Larkin batted in the game's only run during the Twins' time at bat.

Series: 1991 World Series, **Teams and Scores:** Minnesota Twins 4, Atlanta Braves 3

The Twins and Braves both finished in last place in the season prior to their World Series campaigns

Carlton Fisk smashes his "foul pole" clincher for the Red Sox in Game 6

STARTING THE MACHINE

2 The 1975 World Series was shaping up to be a classic after Games 2, 3 and 4 were all decided by a single run, and Game 3 required an extra inning before Joe Morgan batted in the Reds' César Gerónimo. But even though the Reds won the series in Game 7, it's the Red Sox victory in Game 6 that everybody remembers. Cincinnati were gunning for victory, but momentum swung between the two teams. The Red Sox took an early 3-0 lead, but the Reds clawed back and looked on course for victory. The Sox tied it up and had a chance to win in the ninth with the bases loaded, but Johnny Bench's heroics in the field prevented the Red Sox scoring off a Fred Lynn fly ball. When the game went into extra innings at six-apiece, scoring ground to a halt.

In the bottom of the twelfth, Carlton Fisk came to bat for the Red Sox and smashed a pitch down the left-field line. The television cameraman was supposed to follow the flight of the ball, but a rat scurried across his foot and he missed the play. Instead, Americans were treated to the sight of Fisk waving his arms madly as if to alter the flight of the ball. It struck the foul pole and bounced fair into the stands, giving the Sox a walk-off home run – and television viewers witnessed the first 'reaction shot' in baseball history. Directors mimicked the inadvertent mistake in future broadcasts, giving fans a more intimate view of the ballgame.

Series: 1975 World Series, Teams and Scores: Cincinnati Reds 4, Boston Red Sox 3

BREAKING THE CURSE

1 The Yankees had a 3-0 series lead and a one-run advantage in the ninth inning of Game 4 of the 2004 ALCS, until legendary closer Mariano Rivera allowed a stolen base and a single to tie the game. Then Red Sox designated hitter David Ortiz announced his arrival in the series with a home run in the 12th inning that won the game. The comeback had begun.

Game 4 finished so late that Game 5 began just 16 hours later – and this one went even longer. Ortiz was the game winner again, batting in a Johnny Damon run, this time in the 14th inning. In Game 6, Red Sox pitcher Curt Schilling was hampered by a torn tendon sheath. Team doctors had tried to repair it with stitches, but by the end of his seven-inning stint, Schilling's sock was covered in blood. The Yankees missed a trick by not bunting and forcing Schilling to field, and it cost them dearly – they couldn't overturn the four runs that the Red Sox scored in the fourth inning.

With momentum now in their favour, the Red Sox took the deciding Game 7 – the only time that a team came back from a 3-0 series deficit in the postseason. It sparked rapturous celebrations in Boston, but manager Terry Francona knew the job wasn't done yet. The Red Sox carried their good form into the World Series, where they smashed the St Louis Cardinals in four to win their first championship in 86 years. The Red Sox had finally broken the Curse of the Bambino, supposedly placed on the team after they sold Babe Ruth to – who else – the Yankees in 1920.

Series: **2004 American League Championship Series, Teams and Scores: Boston Red Sox 4, New York Yankees 3**

The tight, to-and-fro 2004 ALCS saw several games go late into the night

LL
FRESNO
LOU'S
FRESNO